P9-CEM-077

"In these times of trouble, terror and confusion, we need guidance more than ever about how to ensure that humanity's struggle for its basic rights will continue to advance. *Tainted Legacy* provides that thoughtful guidance, dealing with the practical and ethical dilemmas that we all need to confront if we are not to succumb to the tyranny of the powerful, who would use our fears to trample on the lives of those who are weaker and, apparently, dispensable."

—Ariel Dorfman

"This timely book demonstrates that the war on terrorism can never be won without a renewed commitment to human rights. This compelling volume also makes clear that the idea of national sovereignty must be modified by an increased acceptance of the moral principles of the international community. For everyone struggling to cope with 9/11 this very readable volume will be profound, persuasive and powerful."

—Robert F. Drinan

"*Tainted Legacy* is the most powerful book I have read since September 11th. William Schulz's pragmatic approach to human rights eloquently illustrates how the policies of George. W. Bush and his assault on civil liberties and human rights have made America less, not more secure. He addresses the ambivalence and ambiguity that Americans have displayed from their puritan days to the present toward their own "natural liberties" and the human rights of others. It is a must-read book that helps us better understand how to surmount the threats we are facing in the world since September 11."

—Bianca Jagger

ABOUT THE AUTHOR

William F. Schulz has been executive director of Amnesty International USA since 1994. In that capacity, he travels widely on behalf of human rights and appears frequently in the media. He was described in *The New York Review of Books* as the person who "has done more than anyone else in the American human rights movement to make human rights issues known in the United States." An ordained Unitarian Universalist minister, he served as president of the Unitarian Universalist Association of Congregations from 1985 to 1993.

TAINTED LEGACY

9/11 and the Ruin of Human Rights

WILLIAM F. SCHULZ

Thunder's Mouth Press • Nation Books
New York

To Taylor and Thomas
that their world may be both safe *and* just

• • •

TAINTED LEGACY:
9/11 and the Ruin of Human Rights

Copyright © 2003 William F. Schulz
Preface © 2003 Anthony Lewis

Portions of Chapter Five previously appeared in *The National Interest*.
Portions of Chapter Seven previously appeared in *The Nation*.

Published by
Thunder's Mouth Press/Nation Books
161 William Street, 16th Floor
New York, NY 10038

Nation Books is a co-publishing venture of the Nation Institute
and Avalon Publishing Group Incorporated.

All rights reserved. No part of this publication may be reproduced or transmitted in
any form or by any means, electronic or mechanical, including photocopy, recording,
or any information storage and retrieval system now known or to be invented, without permission in writing from the publisher, except by a reviewer who wishes to
quote brief passages in connection with a review written for inclusion in a magazine,
newspaper, or broadcast.

Library of Congress Cataloging-in-Publication Data is available.

ISBN 1-56025-489-0

9 8 7 6 5 4 3 2 1

Book design by Kathleen Lake, Neuwirth and Associates, Inc.

Printed in the United States of America
Distributed by Publishers Group West

ACC Library Services
Austin, Texas

CONTENTS

PART I RUIN

PART II GROUNDWORK

PART III RECONSTRUCTION

ACKNOWLEDGMENTS

I wrote my first book on human rights, *In Our Own Best Interest: How Defending Human Rights Benefits Us All,* while on a six month sabbatical Amnesty International USA (AIUSA) had generously granted me in the fall of 1999 and winter of 2000. This book I wrote while pursuing full time my regular responsibilities as Executive Director of Amnesty, one of the most complex nonprofit organizations in the country. I don't recommend the latter course but public events wouldn't wait for my next sabbatical. I don't think my duty to Amnesty was compromised by the project but my peace of mind certainly was as I devoted every spare moment for eight months to reading and writing for the book.

Two people in particular are responsible for whatever semblance of equilibrium I may have managed to display during that period—

my wife, Beth Graham, who is expert at maintaining the finely tuned machine that is her husband, and my assistant, Mary Anne Feeney, who is an absolute whiz at finding the answer to any question almost before I even knew I needed to ask it. Mary Anne was the principal researcher for the book and devoted hours to tracking down details even as she expertly fulfilled her customary tasks, such as reminding me that it was Lincoln, Nebraska, to which I was headed as I sprinted for the airport. Beth and Mary Anne are the recipients of my bounteous gratitude, as are others who took on research tasks, including Valeria Scorza and Justin Mazzola.

Much of what I have written here reflects, not surprisingly, the influence of the organization for which I have been privileged to work for the past nine years. But I should say quite explicitly that in many instances the text does *not* reflect the opinions or policies of Amnesty International (AI) and in a few instances it contradicts them. No one should consider this book an official statement on behalf of AI or AIUSA, despite the fact that I have benefited enormously in its preparation from conversations with Irene Khan, AI's Secretary General in London; Paul Hoffman, chair of the AI International Executive Committee and a distinguished human rights lawyer from southern California; Curt Goering, AIUSA's Senior Deputy Executive Director; Charles Brown, Deputy Executive Director for Action Mobilization, Alex Arriaga, Director of our Government Relations Office in Washington, DC; and Rachel Ward, Director of Research.

Mort Winston, Honorary Chair of the AIUSA Board of Directors and Professor of Philosophy at the College of New Jersey in Trenton, NJ, has been an intellectual mentor and kindly read and critiqued several chapters, as did Prof. Sharon Welch of the University of Missouri at Columbia and Prof. Jules Lobel of the University of Pittsburgh School of Law. Needless to say, I appreciated but didn't take all their good counsel so they bear no responsibility for my foolish ways. Nor does Karen Schneider, AIUSA's Deputy Executive

Director for Communications, who read the manuscript cover to cover for editorial purposes and made many helpful suggestions, only about half of which I accepted. But then Karen is a good enough friend that I am only slightly offended when she tells me that a sentence I had thought as powerful as, say, Niagara Falls, was in fact an exhausted metaphor that really ought to be retired.

Carl Bromley, my editor at Nation Books, has been a jewel, not least because he insists on discussing business over sumptuous meals, about which he gets no argument from me. I am also grateful to Carl's assistant, Ruth Baldwin, my agent, Chris Calhoun, and the editor of *The Nation* magazine, Katrina vanden Heuvel, whose grace and kindness convinced me to publish with Nation Books in the first place.

Finally, I want to applaud all my colleagues in the larger human rights community, with a word of special appreciation for Mike Posner of the Lawyers Committee for Human Rights, Len Rubenstein of Physicians for Human Rights, and Felice Gaer of the Blaustein Institute, whose generosity of spirit and devotion to justice provide a model that all who care about human beings might well seek to emulate. None of them will agree with all that I have written—in particular, they probably won't like chapter 8—but their righteousness is well enough tempered by mercy that I don't expect to be cast out of the fraternity/sorority for my heresy.

—Bill Schulz
June 20, 2003

One of the striking developments in world politics over the last three decades has been the revolution of human rights. It is a revolution of expectations, a spreading belief that every human being is entitled to be treated with a basic respect for body and soul: not to be silenced, tortured, brutalized or killed by those in power.

Americans played a crucial part in making respect for human rights a vital doctrine. The administration of President Jimmy Carter made it a formal element in United States foreign policy. Congress tied foreign aid, military and economic, to the human rights record of recipient governments. Yet there is an element in the United States that seems to regard human rights as an unimportant concern for a superpower, something to be doled out as a matter of noblesse oblige when—and only when—it does not get in the way of such serious concerns as American security and prosperity.

That condescending view of human rights gets it exactly backward, and William F. Schulz explains why in his compelling book. Sticking firmly to the demand for human rights is good for American security, indeed crucial. When we close our eyes to official savagery, we endanger our influence in the world, and our safety.

Bill Schulz is what could be called a tough-minded advocate of human rights. There is nothing sentimental about his argument. For example, he describes surprising an audience largely opposed to the war in Iraq by saying he was not against military intervention "in the service of human rights if the odds are good that such intervention will stop more suffering than it will cause." (That is my view, too. The trouble with the Bush Administration's Iraq policy was that the administration was not honest about why it wanted war and then was not prepared to deal with the mess after the war.)

Bosnia is a perfect example of the need for a tough human rights policy. While the Bosnian Serbs slaughtered their Muslim neighbors, Europeans wrung their hands but did nothing. The Clinton Administration, after much evasive dawdling, intervened with force and promptly brought the slaughter to an end. "Human Rights are not for the faint of heart," Schulz writes; "they are not the province of wimps but the stubborn and the robust."

The thrust of this book—the alarming thrust—is to show how the United States has backed away from human rights principles since the terrorist attacks of September 11, 2001. That has happened abroad and at home.

Abroad, the Bush Administration has embraced tyrants on the grounds that they have promised to fight terrorism. Such unsavory regimes as those in Uzbekistan and Kazakhstan are paraded as democratic allies. Cynicism is thick on the ground. President Nursultan Nazarbayev of Kazakhstan uses torture against ethnic opponents. President Bush received him in the White House, and they issued a joint statement declaring their "mutual commitments to advance the rule of law and promote freedom of religion and other universal human rights." In the next six months, twenty newspapers in Kazakhstan were shut down by Nazarbayev, and opposition leaders beaten.

The message sent to the Muslim world by such disregard for the values of human rights is hypocrisy: the United States preaches democracy and law, but in practice it endorses tyranny over Muslim populations. Schulz's point, not difficult to grasp, is that such policy breeds anti-American feelings—and promotes rather than hurts terrorism.

At home, the Bush Administration has determinedly rejected the constraints of the Constitution and its Bill of Rights—the first great American formulation of human rights—as impediments to the war on terrorism. Attorney General John Ashcroft has all but said that the end justifies any means used. When his own Justice Department Inspector General criticized the treatment of aliens detained in a sweep after 9/11, Ashcroft said he would continue to use the same methods.

Schulz gives a chilling example of how aliens were brutalized under the Ashcroft policy. Anser Mehmood, a Pakistani who had overstayed his U.S. visa, was held for six months in a Brooklyn detention center, beaten, mocked, humiliated, finally deported. He had nothing to do with terrorism. The F.B.I. did not even question him after one day. Attorney General Ashcroft said his policy helped keep America safe. To the contrary, it could only create bitterness and hatred of America in Anser Mehmood and his family and others who came to what they viewed as a land of opportunity and justice.

U.S. leaders, past and present, have spoken often of their desire to spread democracy in the world. But it has become increasingly clear that democracy in the sense of a ballot, without more, is an insufficient concept. Many developing countries have had elections but remain societies subject to the whim, and cruelty, of rulers. What is necessary for a true democracy is the rule of law, which means respect for individual rights. Aharon Barak, president of the Supreme Court of Israel, put it succinctly: "Democracy," he said, "cannot exist without the protection of individual human rights."

That is the lesson that the United States should be teaching in the world: teaching by example.

INTRODUCTION "I don't ever want to speak English again"

A few days after September 11, 2001, the FBI arrested 10 percent of the largest community of Mauritanians in the United States, an enclave of immigrants living in the river counties between Louisville, Kentucky, and Cincinnati, Ohio. One of those arrested was Cheik Melainine ould Belai, the twenty-year-old son of a Mauritanian diplomat.

Ould Belai's name was not destined to find its way into the annals of the war on terror. He was not a John Walker Lindh or a Zacarias Moussaoui, much less a Mohammad Atta. He was in fact what he tried to tell the authorities he was: the son of a respected Mauritanian family who had come to the United States to visit family and friends. But ould Belai's English was limited, and the officials

1

provided no translator. So for more than a month he was shuttled between detention centers from Kentucky to Louisiana.

Then, forty days after he was apprehended, ould Belai was released. He had never been told why he had been detained but, whatever the reason, he had been transferred repeatedly from one facility to another, often without notice to his lawyer; provided limited contact with his family; and generally humiliated. Was it because he had overstayed his tourist visa for six weeks—an offense that, prior to September 11, would almost certainly not have resulted in his incarceration? Or was it because an anonymous tipster had informed the F.B.I. erroneously that he had gone to flight school? Was it because of the number of entry stamps from Qatar in his passport, a result of visits to his family when his father was posted there? Or was it simply because he was Mauritanian, a Muslim, at a time in American history when that was the wrong thing to be?

Ould Belai was not to know. Within a short time he was deported for the visa violation—something the government had every legal right to do. But before he left, ould Belai had one last thing to say, a parting coda: "I used to like the United States," he observed, more in sadness and puzzlement than hostility. "Now I don't understand it. I was going to learn English, but now I don't want to ever speak it again."[1]

The treatment meted out to ould Belai is emblematic of the approach the United States has taken to the threat of terrorism over the past two years. What happened to the young man could have been far worse, of course. Ould Belai was not tortured and was ultimately released. But the fact that he was picked up in the first place, largely, it appears, because of his ethnic origin, and held for weeks without knowing why—a violation of international standards for the treatment of detainees[2]—was destined to alienate him, his family, his community and perhaps even the Mauritanian government (his father, after all, was part of that government) from the United States and all that it represents. And alienating people who had previously looked upon the United States with admiration and respect, who had wanted to emulate our traditions and learn the English language—this was no way to make the world a safer place for Americans. This was no way to conduct the war against terror.

And yet what if ould Belai *had* been a terrorist or connected with terrorism? What if by taking him into custody, the authorities had prevented another slaughter? Isn't the shaving of some legal and political niceties more than justified? Surely, protecting the lives of hundreds of innocent people is more important than inconveniencing one young man for a little over a month? What are the authorities—who are no more or less perfect than the rest of us—to do? Can we expect them to read the minds of their suspects to determine who is really dangerous and who is not? How are they to go about their job of fighting terrorism—a terribly important job; perhaps the most important they have—without occasionally at least rubbing up against the oh-so-pristine standards of human rights? Where is the balance, in other words, between fighting terror and respecting human rights? Are the two really so at odds with one another?

These are the kind of questions that ought to haunt any of us who work in the human rights field because they embody an age-old quandary: how do we reconcile practice with principle, reality with ideal, pragmatics with absolutes?

When I was a sophomore in high school, I became acquainted with a religious movement that called itself Moral Rearmament. I didn't know a lot about the organization—I didn't know, for example, that its founder, Frank Buchman, had notoriously said in a 1936 interview, "I thank heaven for a man like Adolf Hitler who built a front line of defense against the anti-Christ of Communism"; I only knew that here was a group of people who seemed to share a strong commitment to a clear set of values. Moral Rearmament preached absolute moral standards. An adherent was to practice the four virtues and to practice them uncompromisingly: absolute honesty, absolute purity, absolute unselfishness, and absolute love. For a fourteen-year-old whose great hero, John F. Kennedy, had been killed the year before and who was struggling with emerging issues of identity and sexuality, ethics, and religion, this formula seemed eminently sensible. Simplicity itself. I would become a practitioner of Moral Rearmament. And for a few weeks I did.

For those few weeks, I tried never to lie to my parents or teachers. I tried to vanquish every impure thought from my head. I tried to be generous to a fault. And I tried to adopt an attitude of beatific love toward all of God's creatures. But gradually it began to dawn on me that two or more of these absolute principles might occasionally be in conflict with one another. Absolute honesty, in particular, seemed perpetually at odds with the other virtues. Because she had always had irregular teeth, for example, my mother was occasionally stricken with bad breath. When she was plagued by this condition and wanted me to give her a kiss, ought I do the loving and unselfish thing: simply pucker up and forget it? Or should I do the honest thing and tell her to get her teeth fixed or at least indulge in a swash of Lavoris?

Those impure thoughts were a problem, too. How honest was it of me to think that I could ever banish them entirely? But if I took the path of absolute honesty and just accepted them as a natural part of my adolescent horniness, I would be condemned to violate the injunction against lustfulness. Pretty soon the appeal of Moral Rearmament began to fade. I persuaded myself that its ideas, noble as they might be, were philosophically bankrupt, and I would need to abandon them for the sake of intellectual consistency. (That this allowed me to resume my sexual fantasizing guilt-free might also have had something to do with it.)

At a relatively early age, therefore, I learned the hard truth that a set of injunctions, all of which are to be enforced in equal measure are bound to get in each other's way. If all ten of the Ten Commandments are to be practiced at all times and with equal fervor, what am I to do if my father or mother commands me to kill or to steal? How may I pay them the honor one commandment requires of me if I disobey their instructions to break another? What shall I do if the job I hold to support my aged parents (and in that way to honor them) requires that I break the rule about working on the Sabbath? One need not go as far as some of my fellow theological students and I did when we were studying for the ministry and concluded (for a day or two) that the only defensible philosophical position was "Ambiguism" (by which we meant that nothing could be proclaimed with certainty) to recognize that ethical systems based on absolute rules are absolutely impossible to implement.

This insight is an important one for human rights because the Universal Declaration of Human Rights (UDHR), the premier articulation of the fundamental rights that any human being may claim, contains more than thirty of them. What happens when one of those rights comes in conflict with another? Article 18, for example, guarantees everyone the freedom "either alone or in community with others and in public or private, to manifest his religion or belief in . . . . practice." But what happens if my religious practice requires violation of Article 16's insistence that "men and women . . . are entitled to equal rights as to marriage, during marriage and at its dissolution?" Which right trumps the other? Human rights advocates often act as if various human rights claims fit together seamlessly, but this is in fact far from true.

And nothing has dramatized the conflict more, the conflict between different rights, than the war on terrorism. Article 3 of the UDHR provides that "everyone has the right to . . . security of person." Being safe from terrorism is not just a nice idea; it is our *right* as human beings, every bit as important a right as any other. Indeed, some might well argue it is our most important right since, if we are dead, we can hardly claim any of the others.

The United States government has contended that in some cases the release at a public trial of sensitive intelligence information about terrorism might jeopardize the public's safety. If the government's claims are true, how do we reconcile the "security right" of Article 3 with the "liberty right" of Article 10 that insists that those charged with crimes must receive a "public hearing"? If we consider human rights the equivalent of absolute rules, we have here a classic example of incompatible absolutes.

But of course human rights do not in most cases constitute absolute rules, much as we in the human rights community often make it sound as if they do. Some rights are, indeed, uncompromisable (the fancy legal term is "nonderogable"), the right not to be tortured being perhaps the most commonly agreed upon such right—at least in principle. But many rights can justifiably be reinterpreted, modified, and even suspended, depending upon circumstances. In this respect human rights are like religious injunctions—"Love thy neighbor as thyself"; "Eat only cloven-footed animals that chew their cuds"; "Pray facing Mecca five times a day." They start out sounding simple but, once the interpreters get hold of them, you would think Jesus, Yahweh, and Muhammad were tax accountants. The great Swiss theologian, Karl Barth, was once asked to summarize his immense four-volume *magnum opus* called *Church Dogmatics*. "What I was trying to say," he replied, "was that 'Jesus loves me/This I know/'Cause the Bible/Tells me so.'"

Fortunately, the UDHR provides us some guidance in deciding priorities among competing rights. Article 29 tells us that rights are subject "only to such limitations . . . determined by law solely for the purposes of securing due recognition and respect for the rights and freedoms of others and *of meeting the just requirements of morality, public order, and the general welfare in a democratic society*." This is the international equivalent of Supreme Court Justice Arthur J. Goldberg's famous remark that, for all its guarantees of freedom, "The Constitution is not a suicide pact."[3] Rights may be limited to secure "public order and the general welfare in a democratic society," to protect us against, say, terrorism[4]. Those are the only purposes for which limitations are allowed in the UDHR, but they are in fact allowed. The critical questions then become both "How many limitations?" and "Are they wise?"

If we accept the United States government's pleas, the answer to the first question is "Many."[5] If we accept the opinion of many human rights analysts, the answer is "Few."[6] But the government has not stopped to consider the full implications of the compromise of human rights, not least for the success of the war on terror. And the human rights community has not provided an adequate strategy for fighting terrorism while still maintaining optimal respect for human rights. The first failing is dangerously shortsighted. The second is profoundly irresponsible. And between them, they may well lead a casual observer to conclude that our right to security and the protection of other rights really *are* irreconcilable. In fact nothing could be further from the truth.

Shortly following the 9/11 attacks, many Americans concluded that they would be prepared to give up some of their rights and liberties if to do so would make the world a safer place to live. In polls conducted in November 2001, strong majorities favored giving law enforcement broader authority to do such things as wiretap telephones (68 percent); intercept mail (57 percent); and detain suspects for a week without charging them (58 percent). Sixty-eight percent supported the government being able to listen in on conversations between terrorist suspects and their lawyers. Sixty-one percent believed that anyone who supports terrorism should not be allowed to give a speech at a college, and only 57% defended the speech-giving rights of someone who believes that terrorism is the

fault of how our country behaves in the world[7]. Assassinations of foreign leaders in the course of the war on terrorism got a nod of
approval from 60 percent of those surveyed, and 32 percent even
supported the torture of terror suspects.[8]

Yet at the same time Americans expressed qualms about sacrificing rights. Nearly two-thirds (65 percent) are concerned that such
broader powers will be used against innocent people and that they
themselves—or people they know and respect—are likely to have to
give up some rights and liberties (58 percent).[9]

None of these numbers—on either side of the question—have
changed appreciably in the ensuing months. The ambivalence they
represent is hardly surprising. Americans are taught almost from
their first days in school that ours is a "sweet land of liberty" that
protects freedom both at home and around the world. But if our liberties put us in greater danger of dying, only a fool—or Patrick
Henry—would choose death. And perhaps it is worth noting that
Patrick Henry lived more than twenty years after uttering those
immortal words "Give me liberty or give me death" and died comfortably in his bed.

That Americans are so willing to sacrifice their rights and those of
others around the world reflects both the fear our leaders have
instilled in us (terrorists "go to school," Secretary of Defense Donald
Rumsfeld has said, on the vulnerabilities of an open society)[10] and
the failure of those of us who support human rights to explain adequately how protecting them, both at home and abroad, actually
makes terrorism less likely to succeed rather than more. It also
reflects a deep-seated confusion about what human rights are and
why they are important.

This book is designed to do three things. First, to make the case
to policy makers and those who influence them that the war on terrorism will never be won absent a renewed commitment to respect
for human rights. Second, to challenge supporters of human rights

to recognize that the reality of terrorism requires us to rethink some of our most sacred assumptions. And third, to answer some of the tough questions about human rights that have been thrown into bold relief by the events of 9/11 and their aftermath,

As executive director of Amnesty International USA for the past nine years, I have spoken to and taken questions from literally thousands of people. From the war-ravaged streets of Monrovia, Liberia, to the barricades of Belfast, Northern Ireland. From snooty sophomores at the Yale Political Union to left wing nuts at Carroll College in Helena, Montana ("Given your criticisms of Fidel Castro's human rights record, Dr. Schulz, I can only conclude that you are a secret CIA operative.") From right-wing fanatics at Pepperdine University in Malibu ("Given your kind words for Fidel Castro's education and literacy programs, Dr. Schulz, I can only conclude that you are an unrepentant Bolshevik.") to the sweet innocents of Pittsburg State University in Kansas, who wouldn't know right-wing from left. From prisoners at the Maricopa County Jail in Phoenix, Arizona, to corporate chieftains at Texaco headquarters in Westchester County, New York (I do not say this for effect but the prisoners truly *did* have better questions). On *Politically Incorrect* (may it rest in peace), *Larry King Live*, *Crossfire,* and in a half dozen sparring episodes with Bill O'Reilly. ("You know, Bill," O'Reilly told me at a cocktail reception once, "I agree with your opposition to the death penalty. Only I oppose it because I think it's too good for these bums. I'd just set them loose on an iceberg somewhere up in Alaska and let them fend for themselves." Which means, if you follow the "logic," that O'Reilly must want them to suffer a series of privations but, since he "opposes" the death penalty, eventually to escape and go scot-free.)

Yet no matter the setting, four or five basic questions are likely to pop up at one time or another. Questions like "Where do human rights come from anyway?" Or "What right do we have to impose our values on others?" Or "Aren't you human rights folks asking us

Americans to give up our sovereignty?" Or "Sure, but what if by torturing a prisoner we could get information that would save hundreds
of innocent lives?"

This book will offer some straightforward answers to these questions, because if Americans remain as unclear about these issues as
they appear to be now, the goal of building a truly human rights-
respecting culture in this country will remain a distant vision. And
that, as I have said, would make our world a far more dangerous one
in which to live.

In February 2002, Michael Ignatieff, head of the Carr Center for
Human Rights at Harvard's Kennedy School of Government and a
respected human rights scholar, wrote an editorial in the *New York
Times* titled "Is the Human Rights Era Ending?" "In the Reagan
years, the [human rights] movement merely risked being unpopular," Ignatieff observed. "In the Bush era, it risks irrelevance." *If.* If
it does not "challenge directly the claim that national security
trumps human rights." And *if* it fails to recognize that respect for
human rights cannot be bought at the cost of a country's stability,
that "nobody's rights . . . will be furthered if [a] state collapses into
anarchy or fundamentalist absolutism," and that human rights advocates must work just as hard against that as we do against a sitting
government's abuses.[11]

Many of my colleagues were upset with Ignatieff. He had over-
stated the case, overlooked this point or that. But I thought he had
it exactly right. We *do* need to explain how respect for human rights
increases our security rather than jeopardizes it. And we *do* need to
recognize that human rights are not like flowers or artwork; they are
not good in and of themselves. They are only good to the extent that
they help us build a better world.

Ultimately the question every one of us human rights advocates
must answer is this: Will more people die if we follow human rights
standards or if we modify or even violate them? Sometimes it is

impossible to know for sure. Obviously I wouldn't be in the business I'm in if I didn't think that the vast majority of the time the answer is that far more will suffer or die if human rights standards are ignored than if they are abided by. But we simply must, particularly in the face of terrorism, be willing to ask ourselves the question and be as clear as we can in the answer. This book is my attempt to address that challenge.

PART I RUIN

CHAPTER 1

"Terrorists are the fish; the people are the sea"[12]

The Demystification of Terrorism

I have often been asked to be fair and to view a matter from all sides. I did so, hoping that something might improve if I viewed all sides of it. But the result was the same. So I went back to viewing things only from one side, which saves me a lot of work and disappointment.

Karl Kraus

If there is one thing I know something about, it is evil. I know about it in theory, and I know about it from direct experience.

I know about it in theoretical terms because I studied theology, a field in which evil is one of the two or three Big Topics. Why do bad things happen to good people? Why does an all-powerful God permit evil in the world?

And I know about it directly from my work with Amnesty International, in which I am exposed to evil virtually every day of my life. I see its consequences in the disfigured face of a ten-year-old girl, scarred for life when the much older man to whom she had been married off by her family threw acid into her eyes to punish her for some minor disobedience. I know it in its purest form in the soldier who makes sport of killing pregnant women by extracting their fetuses from their bellies and tossing the fetuses into the air to see if he can spear them on his bayonet. And I meet it masquerading as civility when I shake the hand of the government minister who I know has ordered the torture and execution of hundreds.

Nothing can excuse atrocities such as these. No appeal to cultural differences can excuse the husband. No lack of oversight by his commander can exonerate the soldier. No pursuit of a political agenda can explain away the actions of the minister. Evil is real and it is very important to call it by its name. When President Bush labeled those who terrorized Americans on September 11, 2001 "evildoers," he was absolutely right, and his instinct to avenge their deaths was, too.

The Hindu ascetic Sri Ramakrishna was once asked why God allowed evil to flourish and he replied, "To thicken the plot." Well, the plot has by now become quite thick enough, thank you, thoroughly convoluted. And one way to untangle it is to be as clear as possible about behavior that falls outside the bounds of the acceptable. This is part of what human rights are all about. Human rights are designed to make the world a safer place and to help stop people from doing evil things. Terrorists may sincerely think that what they are doing is good, but advocates of human rights have no problem agreeing with the president: Terrorist acts are evil and terrorists must be punished.

• • •

Rachel Levy died for want of a bunch of parsley. That was what the seventeen-year-old Israeli girl was seeking, that and coriander and red pepper to flavor the fish her mother was preparing, the afternoon she died. When she rushed into the supermarket in the southern Jerusalem neighborhood of Kiryat Hayovel on March 29, 2002 she barely noticed the Palestinian girl, herself only eighteen, though the two brushed against each other in the entranceway. And then the Palestinian, Ayat al-Akhras, pressed the detonator to the explosives strapped around her waist, and she and Rachel Levy became permanently entwined in the embrace of history.

Rachel left a legacy of flowing hair and a gap between her teeth, pop music, poetry, and Tommy Girl perfume; and an apolitical innocence about the conflict going on around her.

And Ayat? Ayat, too, left a legacy. Of a life spent in the poverty of the Dehaishe refugee camp outside Jerusalem. Of posters of pop stars from Egypt and Iraq. Of ambition to be a journalist. Of a fiancé and wedding plans for the coming summer. But also of hot anger at the Israelis. Of disgust with the passivity of Arab leaders who failed to advance the Palestinian cause. And of rage at the killing of her neighbor, Isa Zakari Faraj, shot dead through a window by the Israeli Defense Forces as he and his daughter played with Legos in the privacy of their home. That was just a few weeks before Ayat connected with the Al Aqsa Martyrs Brigade, a few weeks before they supplied her with the bomb and a few weeks before she and Rachel Levy brushed against each other in a supermarket doorway.[13]

What Ayat did was indefensibly wrong. It was evil. It cannot be excused. No amount of Palestinian suffering and no litany of Israeli offenses can justify Ayat al-Akhras killing Rachel Levy. And those who encouraged Ayat and supplied her with the weaponry deserve to be punished. It is important to say all this.

The only remaining question is, if we want to prevent future Ayats from killing other Rachels, is it enough to say all this and to stop?

• • •

No one who read the *New York Times* in the months following 9/11 could fail to notice and be moved by the short biographies of the World Trade Center victims that appeared regularly in that paper. Myrna Yaskulka was a Staten Island grandmother who sported pink rhinestone-studded sunglasses and wore leopard skin pants. Kevin Dowdell was a much-decorated firefighter who sanded floors on his days off to make ends meet. And Christine Lee Hanson was a two-and-a-half-year-old flying with her parents in the plane that crashed into the second tower. These were good people. They were people with whom every one of us could identify. Not one of them asked to be part of a drama. Not one of them knew that their deaths would trigger a worldwide struggle. Not one could have imagined all that their dying would come to mean. Theirs is an honorable legacy.

Since then, we have learned a great deal about Osama bin Laden, but in many ways, the more intriguing figure apparently responsible for all those deaths is Ayman al-Zawahiri. Al-Zawahiri is the reputed "brains" behind the bombings of the American embassies in East Africa in 1998, the attack on the USS *Cole*, and the events of September 11. For many years the head of the Egyptian-based Islamic Jihad, al-Zawahiri was raised in a prominent Islamic family and trained as a medical doctor. Since 1998 he and Islamic Jihad have collaborated with bin Laden and Al Qaeda and in June 2001 the two organizations merged. A bitter enemy of Israel and the United States, al-Zawahiri, now fifty-one, has been a revolutionary since the age of fifteen, eager to see Islamic rule (*shari'a* law) imposed upon Egypt and throughout the Islamic world and without compunction about how that is accomplished. Speaking of the 9/11 hijackers, al-Zawahiri said, "This was not just a human achievement—it was a holy act."

It is certainly possible that al-Zawahiri would have ended up a terrorist mastermind under almost any circumstances. He was always highly devout, politically aware and unbending in his devotion to Islamicism. But what is revealing about his life is that at one turning point after another, whatever inclinations he may have had to take a violent route were reinforced by his encounter with violations of human rights.

His mentor, Sayyid Qutb, the most prominent thinker of the Islamic fundamentalist movement in the 1950s and 1960s, to take but one example, was imprisoned in 1954 along with more than one thousand other members of the Muslim Brotherhood suspected of conspiring to assassinate Egyptian President Gamal Abdel Nasser. Qutb was tortured mercilessly and later hanged. His mistreatment took on the bearing of a legend, earned Qutb status as a martyr, and convinced al-Zawahiri that there was no way to compromise with repressive governments.

That conviction can only have been sharpened when al-Zawahiri went to Pakistan with the Red Crescent Society in 1980 to provide medical care to Afghan refugees, many of them casualties of Soviet land mines, and again later when he was himself tortured while imprisoned for two years in connection with the assassination of Anwar Sadat. One of Egypt's most prominent advocates of democracy, Saad Eddin Ibrahim, speculated that al-Zawahiri emerged from his prison experience with an overwhelming desire for revenge. "Torture does have that effect on people," Ibrahim observed. "Many who turn fanatic have suffered harsh treatment in prison."[14]

None of these experiences mitigates the horror of the crimes of which al-Zawahiri is suspected. None of them prompts even a moment's reconsideration of our desire to call his acts evil. But they do raise the simple question of whether calling something evil is enough.

Because in order to stop evil, to unravel the plot, to adapt Ramakrishna's metaphor, we need to do more than to name it. We need as well to understand it, to see how it was created and survives. For, after all, while the fruits of evil may be obvious, its perpetrators are often quite cunning. Remember the word Genesis uses to describe Eve's tempter? "The serpent," it says, "was subtle."

• • •

To understand the evil that is terrorism, then, we need to understand many things: the psychology of hatred; the dynamics of group

pressure; the appeal of religious extremism; the dangers of economic inequity; the pull of ethnic pride. These and many other factors have been debated endlessly since 9/11. But one thing has been
largely neglected: the relationship between human rights violations
and the birth and perpetuation of terrorism.

Terrorists come, of course, in many shapes and sizes. Terrorism
has deep roots and diverse causes. But one thing its various manifes-
tations almost always have in common is that they have been fueled
by violations of human rights. The Revolutionary Armed Forces of
Colombia (FARC), for instance, the notorious left-wing guerillas,
have managed to replenish their ranks, when they weren't engaging
in forced conscription, by appearing to champion the economic
interests of the impoverished against unyielding landowners and
their allies in government. The Kurdistan Workers' Party (PKK),
while at first alienating many Kurds in Turkey with its radical rhetoric and violent tactics, gradually earned widespread respect, if not
membership, by standing up for the Kurdish minorities' rights to
political and cultural expression. And Sri Lanka's Liberation Tigers of
Tamil Eelam were formed in response to the Sinhalese majority's
persecution of the Tamil minority, including refusing them the right
to vote, to receive a public education, or to use their own language.

Terrorists commit vicious human rights crimes. But they also
thrive on the crimes of others. Eliminating human rights violations
would not stop all terrorism, of course. Terrorism must be combated
on many different levels—by law enforcement, military action, intelligence, financial controls, new technologies, airport security. But far
from being an impediment to a terror-free world, as they have so
often been portrayed in the past two years, human rights are in truth
a benefactor of it.

Granted, human rights take longer to work their magic than a
missile does. But depriving people of their rights feeds terrorism
and any global strategy that overlooks, much less denigrates, their

importance is ultimately bound to fail. Abiding by human rights standards is not sufficient to diminish the threat of terrorism, but it certainly is a necessary condition for achieving that goal.

From the rhetoric U.S. leaders have tendered since 9/11, they sometimes seem to get that. On the first anniversary of that terrible day, President George W. Bush gave eloquent testimony that "America will . . . take the side of brave men and women who advocate human rights and democratic values. . . . The United States will promote moderation, tolerance, and the nonnegotiable demands of human dignity—the rule of law, limits on the power of the state, and respect for women, private property, free speech, and equal justice."[15] But something has gotten lost in the translation.

And part of the reason is because our leaders have been content to condemn terrorism as evil and leave it at that. Such an approach is understandable, of course. We humans feel safer if we can identify the exact location of the demonic in life. That is one reason the death penalty is so popular in the United States—because it assures us that evil, the demonic, is right *there,* embodied in those criminals on death row, and, moreover, that with their annihilation, a part of evil, itself, will thereby be vanquished. To take this tack is comforting. Evil is no longer floating around somewhere out there in the ether (nor, conveniently, is it located inside our own hearts or manifest in our own acts); it is tethered to a select group of very real people committing very real deeds, and all that is required of us is to destroy those people and we will have gone far toward destroying the phenomenon of Evil as well. The only problem with such a strategy is that we risk in the process destroying our own hearts.

For if something is considered overwhelmingly, irredeemably, incomprehensibly evil, the very embodiment of the Satanic, then may we not be justified in using virtually any means to eradicate it? That is certainly how bin Laden and his ilk feel about us. But one reason to conduct ourselves in accordance with the rule of law and respect for the fundamental human rights of even the most despicable among us is in order to complement the anger and anguish we quite understandably experience when we are hurt by evildoers with the wisdom and civility that characterizes the kind of world in which we want some day to live.

A rapist has committed an evil deed and deserves to be punished, but the reason the criminal justice system doesn't allow the rapist to be raped as punishment in return is because we don't want to indulge our basest desires or live in a society that tolerates "state rape." Many criminals may well deserve to be called "evil" or at least the perpetrators of evil deeds, but we do not punish them for *being* evil; we punish them for committing specific, identifiable crimes. Human rights apply to even the worst of us, even the terrorist, the terrorist sympathizer, and certainly to the thousands of people who may be suspected of being terrorists but are not. It is easy to get confused about that but, if we do, our society will end up corrupt and tarnished, and evil will be all that much harder to stop.[16]

• • •

The way to begin, then, to understand the evil of terrorism is to demystify it. Despite the fact that terrorists live largely in the shadows, we actually know quite a bit about them, both generically and specifically of Al Qaeda, and much of what we know goes against the popular grain.

Terrorists are not "insane." We would like to think that they are, of course. We often use the word "insane" in a vernacular sense to describe what they do. It is a way to express our rage and to morally condemn those who cause it. Some terrorists no doubt are clinically pathological. But according to most students of terrorist psychology, the vast majority of terrorists would probably score within the range of "normal" on the Minnesota Multiphasic Personality Inventory

(MMPI). Indeed, as a massive study by the Library of Congress concluded, "psychopaths are too unreliable and incapable of being con-
trolled to be of use to terrorist groups."[17] Even those who are
prepared to commit suicide to further their cause do so usually not
because they are depressed or lack self-esteem (common causes of
suicide in the general population), but because they are convinced
that they are dying for a worthy cause. The Japanese Kamikaze
pilots of World War II were often among the brightest students at
Japanese universities, well read in the likes of Plato, Goethe, and
Shakespeare, and certain that their deaths could save their country
and thereby purify the world.[18]

Terrorists have "rational" goals. This is hard to swallow, I know.
But the point is only that, within the framework of their political or
religious worldview, what terrorists do usually has an internal consistency to it. They are not just people running around causing mayhem for mayhem's sake. They hope to accomplish a set of goals, and
those goals are often quite specific and even sophisticated. The
notion that Al Qaeda undertakes its mission solely because "they
hate us " or because "they wish to destroy freedom" is so naïve as to
be frightening. If they merely wished to "destroy freedom," they
would make Sweden, arguably one of the world's freest countries, a
high priority for attack. Terrorists are wrong-headed, to be sure, but
they are not necessarily muddle-headed. If they were, they might be
less effective. But the upside to the fact that terrorists have
"rational" goals is that they are thereby susceptible to deterrence.
"Always pray that your opposition be [rational]," advised the political theorist Marion J. Levy Jr., because "there is always the possibility, in theory, of handling the [rational] by out thinking them."[19]

Terrorists need support to be successful. This is a critical point.
Terrorists are not in this game for their health. Yes, some believe

they will go to heaven and ogle virgins all night long if they kill enough infidels, but their leaders certainly, the theorists and strategists, have far larger ends in mind. And those "rational" ends depend upon convincing large numbers of people to change their minds. About corrupt leaders. Or about *shari'a* law. Or about the United States. Terrorists have a product to sell and they need to know that they are beating out "Brand X," winning over the undecided.

Moreover, terrorists need the support of large numbers of people simply to operate in the first place. They need, for example, a friendly or indifferent government that tolerates the presence of their training camps and "sleeper cells" and whose citizens make no demands for their ouster. They need financial support and logistical assistance and, most of all, they need a ready pool of new recruits. They need, in other words, a *retinue*. As the Library of Congress study put it, "If [a terrorist operation] fails to recruit new members . . . it is likely to disintegrate. The terrorist groups that have been active for many years have a significant base of popular support."[20] When the father of a young Palestinian suicide bomber reacted to his son's death by saying, "I am proud of what he did. He did it for God and our people," the father was not just displaying a perverse form of bravado: he was signaling how widely the Palestinian population, the vast majority of whom are not themselves terrorists, find the terrorists' cause to be just[21].

Terrorist leaders are often middle class but those to whom they appeal are often not. Much has been made of the fact that Osama bin Laden comes from a wealthy family, that Ayman al-Zawahiri, as we have seen, was trained as a medical doctor, and that the nineteen flyers on 9/11 were all middle class. Daniel Pipes, in particular, has argued that there is no relationship between poverty and militant Islam and that therefore "foreign aid cannot serve as the outside world's main tool to combat it."[22]

It is true that many terrorist leaders and operatives have more than average education and come from middle-class backgrounds.[23] It makes a certain amount of sense that those who conceptualize sophisticated goals and formulate clever strategies will be above average in education and intelligence. Given the complexity of the tools of the terrorist trade today—computers, biochemicals, airplanes—not just any dunderhead can be among the terrorist elite. Then, too, it is a sociological truism that the aspiring and/or alienated middle classes are always the ones that make the revolutions.

But this is certainly not always the case. The infamous Velupillai Prabharakaran, charismatic leader of the Tamil Tigers in Sri Lanka, was a high school dropout.[24] Khalid Shaikh Mohammed, the high-ranking Al Qaeda operative arrested in March 2003 in Pakistan, grew up in what were described as the "dingy immigrant streets" of Kuwait City, "angered by the country's disparities of wealth and privilege."[25] And when it comes to the rank and file, they are often drawn from the underclass. The foot soldiers of both the Protestant and Catholic paramilitaries in Northern Ireland, for example, have been overwhelmingly working class. Indeed, the so-called "Buffalo Six," the young Yemenite men, most of whom have pled guilty to attending an Al Qaeda training camp, are typical of many of those charged with terrorist-related activity in the United States over the last two years: they held low-paying jobs, when they worked at all, in the hardscrabble town of Lackawanna, New York. And the suicide bombers who struck Morocco in May 2003 all grew up in poverty.

The point is that even when the terrorist elite *is* middle class, their followers, their retinue, are often not. Most of the students in the Pakistani religious schools (*madrassas*) who are taught to hold Al Qaeda in reverence and to applaud, if not emulate, its tactics are enrolled in those schools at least in part because their parents are too poor to provide other kinds of education. Alienated young working class Arab men living in France and suffering from widespread discrimination against immigrants there constitute what one sociologist has dubbed "the new martyrs": "easily recruited zealots who are willing to fight, and die, for a religious cause about which, initially, they know very little."[26] And the degradation of Palestinian refugee camps has long been recognized as a breeding ground for suicide bombers. Ayat was hardly atypical. As another Palestinian youngster put it straightforwardly following an Israeli incursion into his camp, "I am so angry I am ready to blow myself up."[27] None of this is to say that poverty alone is sufficient motivation for someone to become a terrorist and, needless to say, the overwhelming majority of the world's poor resist the temptation to violence. But the resentment that deprivation fosters is often the seed of a widespread sympathy.

Because they have limited resources, terrorists depend upon their adversaries to make mistakes. Terrorists know that their adversaries outgun them. Like the character in Joseph Conrad's *The Secret Agent* who wished to destroy pure mathematics but settled for the Greenwich Clock Tower, they know that they cannot accomplish their goals all at once. They may believe they have God on their side and will triumph in the end, but they don't mind a bit if their opponents help them do it by playing their cards badly. And perhaps the most common mistake of the counterterrorists is to believe that repression and force alone will bring the bad guys to bay.

Police and military action are a fully justifiable component of the struggle against terrorism. Indeed, it is hard to see how terrorism will ever be defeated absent the application of a degree of muscle. While many pacifists may also be human rights activists, there is no reason why human rights activists must also be pacifists. Those who commit terrorist crimes must be brought to justice and that usually requires some use of force.

But force alone, especially when it is disproportionate or coupled with political repression, can feed into the terrorists' hands. It is hardly a coincidence that the September 11 attackers emerged out of countries—Saudi Arabia and Egypt—notorious for their repression of political opponents. Or that whenever the United States or its allies, such as Israel or Uzbekistan or certain warlords in Afghanistan, are accused of committing human rights crimes, terrorists exploit those charges to raise further doubts about American motives.

When force is accompanied by perceived insensitivity, the damage is squared. Whether it be identifying itself with corrupt rulers, acting parsimoniously with economic assistance, failing to hold allies to the same human rights standards we apply to adversaries, or appearing to disparage the opinions and interests of the Arab and Muslim world, the United States invites that world's rage. Add to those missteps discriminatory practices against Muslims in the United States, and we reinforce the speculation that the war against terrorism is sparked by anti-Islamic sentiment, thus handing the terrorists a silver bomb on a golden platter.

Terrorism can be diminished by the wise and targeted application of force—that may work in the short term—but ultimately the terrorist fish die off only by the elimination of their support structure, the terrorists' retinue: the people who constitute the sea. To make that happen requires that we give that larger community every reason to reject the terrorist agenda, every reason to isolate the terrorists and help track them down, and as few reasons as possible to doubt the sincerity of our own motives. The United States could make no greater mistake in formulating its strategy to combat terrorism than to assume that respect for human rights has little role to play. The truth is that bringing the criminals to justice and doing so in a just way are two sides of the same coin.

• • •

Building upon these generalizations, we turn now to a consideration of Al Qaeda itself and its affiliated cells and allies. From the millions

of words that have been written about Osama bin Laden and his
henchmen, we can glean a few key conclusions upon which the vast
majority of observers agree.

Al Qaeda is global in its reach. While those at the core of the bin
Laden–al-Zawahiri operation, those who have taken an oath called a
bayat, similar to the Mafia's pledge of *omerta*, promising to follow
their leaders even unto death, may be as few as 200,[28] there is good
reason why that core took for itself the name Al Qaeda, meaning
The Base. For Al Qaeda is in fact the base, the inspiration, if you
will, of a much larger, far flung, loosely related network of terrorist
organizations consisting of between 10,000 and 110,000 recruits and
operating in some eighty countries, united not by a tight command
structure emanating from one center but by common ideology.[29]
When we speak of "Al Qaeda," therefore, we are not just talking
about bin Laden and his immediate associates. (Their deaths alone
would hardly put an end to worldwide terrorism.) We are using
shorthand for a huge conglomerate of sympathetic partisans that
one author has dubbed "Holy War, Inc."[30] If the United States were
to commit military resources to combat Al Qaeda every place in
which it is found, we would be fighting in at least 42 percent of the
countries of the world.[31]

Al Qaeda knows its history. Al Qaeda did not spring full-blown
from the head of Zeus or even, for that matter, of Muhammad. It
traces its intellectual origins back through al-Zawahiri's mentor,
Sayyid Qutb, who railed against a Western plot to dominate Islam, to
the renowned thirteenth-century Muslim reformer, Ahmad ibn
Taymiyya, who declared the Mongol invaders of the Middle East
infidels and apostates despite their having converted to Islam. As
radical *Salifis*, (that is, devotees of the "venerable forefathers," the
Prophet Muhammad and his companions, and hence purists who

regard most of the Islam practiced today as corrupted by idolatry), Al Qaeda takes as its fundamental project the salvation of the *umma*, the universal Islamic community, the entire Islamic world.

And from what does the *umma* need saving? From two things: from their enemies within, the hypocritical Muslim rulers of today in Saudi Arabia, Egypt, Pakistan and elsewhere who profess allegiance to the Prophet but who, like the Mongols of old, are wolves in sheep's clothing; and from the allies and puppet masters of those hypocrites, the Western powers, especially the United States and Israel, who, joined in the wicked "Zionist-Crusader alliance," seek to adulterate Islam and keep the Islamic world in perpetual subjugation, be that economic, territorial, cultural, or military. Ibn Taymiyya warned against the first of these dangers; Qutb against the second, and it is Al Qaeda's mission to see that their prophecies not go unheeded in this generation.[32]

Al Qaeda pushes the hot buttons. Like most radical movements, however, Al Qaeda starts with the disadvantage of preaching a message—revolution, hyperorthodoxy, asceticism, violence—which the vast majority of the *umma* are not prepared to adopt. Contrary to ill-informed right-wing opinion in the United States, the vast majority of Muslims did not applaud when the planes hit their targets on 9/11.[33] While Al Qaeda may claim as many as 110,000 operatives, there are more than one billion Muslims in the world. Cleverly, therefore, Al Qaeda has chosen two targets for its ire—corrupt, repressive leaders and a domineering West—that are bound to resonate even with large segments of the Muslim world that would otherwise reject a radical agenda.

The vast majority of Muslims are keenly acquainted with poverty. Indonesia and Pakistan, for example, two of the most populous Muslim countries, are also among the world's poorest. Even among Arab countries, including oil-rich countries, development lags significantly behind the West. The 2002 United Nations Arab Development Report noted that the Gross Domestic Product of all Arab countries combined is less than that of Spain. Real per capita income for 1975–98 grew by around 0.5 percent per year compared to a global average of 1.3 percent. One in five Arabs lives on less than $2 a day. Even in countries like Saudi Arabia in which capital is abundant, it is closely held among a small ruling elite. Arab unemployment averages around 20 percent and sometimes twice that for the high proportions of the population (55 percent in Egypt and almost 60 percent in Saudi Arabia) under the age of twenty-five.[34] And the phenomenon of a large number of young males walking around without work (they are called the *hayateen* or "men who lean against walls") always makes for volatile possibilities.

Moreover, the U.N. Development Report lays the responsibility for the lack of Arab development squarely at the feet of Arab governments. It is the absence of democracy, lack of good governance, denial of human rights, and lowly status of women (with its attendant waste of human resources) that account for the backwardness of these societies. The Arab region is rated lower than any other for freedom of expression and insistence on public accountability. The result is that, despite the strictures of the Koran regarding honesty and fair dealings in business, Arab countries score abysmally low on Transparency International's Corruption Perception Index. As Prince Bindar, the Saudi ambassador to the United States put it dismissively, "If you tell me that building this whole country . . . we misused or got corrupted with fifty billion, I'll tell you, 'Yes . . . So what? We did not invent corruption. . . .'"[35] And other Muslim countries, including Indonesia and Pakistan, are even more corrupt.[36]

Unemployment, economic stagnation, and widespread looting of the public treasury would be difficult enough for Muslim populations to bear even if they had access to mechanisms through which to regularly replace regimes or voice dissent. But of the fifty-seven member states of the Organization of the Islamic Conference, only Bangladesh and Turkey have managed to sustain democracy over an extended period of time, interrupted though it has been in Turkey by military intervention and common as it still is for unpopular political views to result in jail time, torture, and even death. Absent nonviolent, democratic ways through which people can express frustration, where do they turn to seek political change? It is hardly surprising that they sometimes look with sympathy upon political and religious extremists who offer that most rare of commodities—an alternative vision.

Moreover, many Muslims are painfully aware of the defeats they have suffered throughout their history, from the Crusades through the Mongol invasion, from the establishment of the State of Israel and its series of military victories to the 1991 Persian Gulf War. Once one of the world's most advanced civilizations, Islamic culture has been in retreat now, or so it seems to many Muslims, for close to a thousand years.

Ideally, Al Qaeda would like to see coups or civil wars break out against current Islamic leaders but, whether that happens or not, it is easy for extremists to convince rank and file Muslims (the so-called "street") that in a wide variety of ways, their leaders have failed them.

And it's hardly more difficult to convince them that the United States has been complicit in that failure. In many respects Arab communities start off with a favorable view of the United States—the economic opportunity it offers; the democratic principles it champions; the appealing aspects of American popular culture; its relative lack of corruption.[37] But these attractive features are quickly diluted by other American policies and practices. The allegiance we have long paid to repressive Muslim leaders; the economic dominance we have long maintained; the double standard we appear to have fostered in the Israeli-Palestinian conflict; the neglect we have shown in failing to help resolve the dispute over Kashmir; the presence of, until very recently, U.S. troops in Saudi Arabia; the sanctions we championed against Iraq and now our occupation of that country; the apparent laxness of our moral values; the role women play in Western society—all these, some fairly, some not—are held against the United States.

Little wonder, then, that a recent Gallup poll of public opinion in nine predominantly Muslim countries found strongly negative opinions of the United States. "Ruthless, aggressive, conceited, arrogant" were just some of the labels that respondents found appropriate and most were convinced that Westerners do not respect Arab or Islamic values or treat Arabs and Muslims fairly.[38] Indeed, it is not an uncommon view in Indonesia that the C.I.A. was behind the nightclub bombing in Bali[39] or in the Middle East that Saddam Hussein was a shill for the United States who provided an excuse for Washington to intervene in the region, establish military bases, and steal Arab oil.[40] Nor is it surprising that following U.S. intervention in Iraq, Muslim regard for America and support for the war on terrorism slipped even further, as it did even among our staunchest allies.[41] Al Qaeda has done its best to exploit such alienation and, along with its condemnation of the ruling elites, use it to attract the support, the retinue, the "sea," it requires to keep its business flourishing.

Because it has limited resources, Al Qaeda depends upon its adversaries to make mistakes. Osama bin Laden is reputed to be a very wealthy man and Al Qaeda has successfully utilized the *hawala*, an informal, unregulated, worldwide banking system, to transfer funds to its operatives. But even if it had all the money it could possibly need, Al Qaeda would still face a rash of obstacles—from lack of technical expertise to scarcity of weapons to being constantly on the run—that retard the fulfillment of its strategic objectives. Like all terrorist operations, therefore, it relies in good measure on its adversaries to screw up in order to accomplish its goals.

Much press has been given to the intelligence failures that preceded September 11, to the lapses in our immigration procedures, to our lack of preparedness to meet a biological attack. All these important issues are of a technical nature and can no doubt be fixed through allocation of greater resources and a higher concentration of effort. Much praise has been heaped upon our military capabilities and the improvements in airline security. But in key respects, having largely to do with policy and our posture toward the world, the United States has badly bungled its response to terrorism and in these ways offered Al Qaeda a whole suit of trump cards.

Rohan Gunaratna is widely considered one of the world's leading experts on Al Qaeda. He is uncompromising in his support for a tough-minded approach to terrorism and advocates, for example, "punitive . . . measures aimed at targeting the demand and supply side of Al Qaeda" and "a relentless hunt . . . for [its] leaders, members, collaborators, and supporters." But in a widely cited book published in 2002, Gunaratna also offered this advice about how to defeat the terrorists:

> Of equal importance [to military and law enforcement measures] are resolving Kashmir, Palestine, and other international conflicts where Muslims are affected; redressing grievances and meeting the legitimate aspirations of Muslims; and helping Arab and Muslim states improve the quality of life of their citizens. Above all, Al Qaeda's ideology must be countered, in order to . . . lessen its appeal. . . . A military solution is only one part of a wider strategy of implementing socioeconomic and political reforms. Otherwise, the threat will diminish in the short term but reemerge in the mid-term.[42]

Those wise words have gone largely unheeded since they were written. Indeed, in many respects the United States has done exactly the opposite of what Gunaratna recommended. And the only group that such neglect has served is Al Qaeda itself.

The alternative "ideology" and "socioeconomic and political reforms" Gunaratna says will ultimately defeat Al Qaeda entail such things as spreading economic opportunity and respecting Arab culture. But they also include paying greater honor to human rights, not desecrating them. Human rights, reflecting respect for human life, due process for those who harm us, protection of diverse religious opinions, self-government for the masses, economic welfare, and health care for everyone are anathema to all that Al Qaeda stands for. Osama bin Laden knows that and that is why one of his goals is to destroy the solidarity of the international community and undermine the norms and standards that have sustained that community since the end of World War II. That is one reason he has included the U.N. among the objects of his ire. He knows that a world in which human rights were not only a watchword but a reality would be one in which it would be far harder for him to recruit and operate. That is why they and the structures that sustain them have to go. The great irony of the post–9/11 world is that, when it comes to human rights, the United States has been doing bin Laden's work for him.

CHAPTER 2 "Let them hate as long as they fear"

Oderint dum metuan (Caligula)

History and Hubris

Even a superpower needs all the friends it can get to fight terrorism. You don't get that kind of help because you demand it or act unilaterally or thumb your nose at people. You get that kind of cooperation because people want to help you.

Brent Scowcroft, National Security Advisor to President George H. W. Bush

From Puritan days to the present, Americans have displayed a persistent ambivalence about human rights. Inspired by the Pilgrims' quest for religious freedom, the brave affirmations of rights contained in the Declaration of Independence and the Bill of Rights, the blood shed in the Civil War by those seeking an end to human bondage, the defense of freedom in Europe, the leadership provided the U.N., the struggle to extend civil rights to all Americans and the victory over totalitarianism in the Cold War, we have seen ourselves, not without reason, as the world's great champion of democracy and self-government, human rights, and human liberty. But that record, admirable as elements of it are, is not without its ambiguity, a condition that obtained from the very beginning of European settlement on this continent. For quite apart from the injustices meted out to the Native American population, Puritan society contained at its heart contradictions that were to roil American history in one form or another for 350 years.

Emboldened to seek a new land to escape religious persecution, the Puritans did so not to establish a commonwealth of toleration, not to offer to others that of which they had been deprived, but rather to create a society in which their one and only truth—God's Truth— could rule forever. Here is the earliest origin of the idea that ours is an exceptional nation. John Winthrop called it a "city set on a hill," the eyes of all people to be upon it that "men shall say of succeeding plantations, 'The Lord make it like that of New England.'"[43] This was to be a "dictatorship not of a single tyrant . . . but of the holy and regenerate," in the words of the renowned historian of Puritanism, Perry Miller, those who could prove before the church that they possessed the signs of grace. Such a government brooked no dissent and trimmed no policy to the desires of the people.[44] Had the Puritans been strong enough to defeat their adversaries in England and impose a similar theocracy there, no Puritan is likely ever to have set foot on the New World's soil. And when dissenters such as Roger Williams set foot on theirs—"I do affirm it to be against the testimony of Christ Jesus for the civil state to impose upon the soul of the people a religion, a worship, a ministry," he declared impoliticly[45]— they knew what to do with him: they banished him from the colony in the dead of winter, the persecuted transformed into the tyrannous. (It did not help Williams' cause that he opposed the Colony's seizing the lands of the Indians without remuneration.)

Yet enmeshed in Puritan political theory was the notion that government, though it exists to propagate God's Word, is derived from a covenant the people make voluntarily with the Lord and with each other, electing their leaders and renouncing their own "natural liberty" so long as their governors be "good, just, and honest." This was democracy in embryo, to be sure, but it was a democracy subject to ample limitation, for it was only the sanctified and elect who could participate in that social compact. Those deemed insufficiently holy—sometimes dubbed "the inhabitants"—had no voice and no vote. As the minutes of an early New England town meeting are said to have read: "Voted first that the Earth is the Lord's and the Fullness thereof. Voted second that the Earth is given to the Saints. Voted third that *We* are the Saints."

The history of human rights in America begins with a dash for freedom that turned into a vehicle for repression (of both the indigenous population and the apostates in the Puritan community) and an impulse for democracy that foundered on the notion that rights can be denied to the unworthy. That the New World was to be a moral beacon to the globe, a model of righteousness for others to follow, the setter of standards and, as such, that which may take exception to the rules when it is convenient, has also complicated the picture, prompting both a degree of leadership and generosity that has inspired the world and a sense of privilege and self-righteousness that has repelled it. Ought we to lead by example or to impose our system and values, directly or covertly, on others? Must we, like others, be subject to external controls or may we be relied upon to abide by our principles voluntarily? All these paradoxes have long plagued America and continue to describe the tension over human rights to this day.

• • •

In few periods of American history was that tension more manifest than the Revolutionary. Thomas Jefferson's ringing declaration of the self-evident truths that "all men are created equal" and "endowed by their Creator with certain unalienable rights," including "life, liberty, and the pursuit of happiness" founded a nation. Following Puritan polity and such inspirations as John Locke's *Essays on Civil Government* (1690), the Founders acknowledged

that these "unalienable rights" might be surrendered to government
to the degree necessary to create a civil and safe community. But the
American experiment tipped decisively toward less surrender and
more liberty, tipped more emphatically in that direction, indeed,
than any other society yet created.

It did so, however, with one important caveat: that freedom
could only be sustained in tandem with virtue, that a society could
afford to allow a wide exercise of rights only if its people maintained order and respected one another. If they did not, government had an obligation to reassert its authority. The distinguished
historian of early American political thought, Clinton Rossiter,
explained the Founders' thinking this way: "It takes more than a
perfect plan of government to preserve ordered liberty. Something
else is needed . . . : a virtuous people. Men who are virtuous may
aspire to liberty, prosperity, and happiness; men who are corrupt
may expect slavery, adversity, and sorrow."[46]

Little wonder, then, that the United States has displayed such a
streak of overweening moralism throughout its history and even less
that the principle that all men are created equal could coexist so
comfortably for so long beside the institution of slavery. For while
liberty may be an unalienable right, it is (shades of Puritanism) a
right reserved for the worthy. Jefferson, himself a slave owner,
caught the contradiction when he claimed, in respect to the "pecu-
liar institution," to "tremble for my country when I recognize that
God is just," but Jefferson, who was, after all, the Declaration's
author, took its principles more seriously than most. Eighty years
after the Declaration was written, many Americans found it hard to
believe that its words were to be followed literally. Rufus Choate dis-
missed them as "glittering . . . generalities" useful only in a "fool's
paradise" and John C. Calhoun spoke for far more than just
Southerners when he wrote:

> It is a great and dangerous error to suppose that all people are equally entitled to liberty. It is a reward to be earned, not a blessing to be gratuitously lavished on all alike—a reward reserved for the intelligent, the patriotic, the virtuous, the deserving—and not a boon to be bestowed on a people too ignorant, degraded, and vicious, to be capable either of appreciating or enjoying it.[47]

Even the Civil War was fought as much, if not more, to preserve the union than to free the slaves, and when Stephen A. Douglas declared that he "would not blot out the great inalienable rights of the white men for all the Negroes in the world," Abraham Lincoln replied that Douglas was "blowing out the moral lights around us" but appealed ultimately to the pragmatic argument that "a house divided against itself cannot stand."[48]

To subsume liberty to order, to predicate the bestowal of freedom and human rights upon the worthiness of their recipients, to endorse a limited government while trusting that government to measure well any limitations it sets on its citizens—these have been characteristic struggles within the American soul since the country's birth. They have been reflected in a John Adams who could both say that "a free press maintains the majesty of the people" and champion the Sedition Act that threatened five years in prison to anyone whose opinions besmirched the good name of a government official or sowed confusion among the people.[49] They make their appearance in an Abraham Lincoln who could speak eloquently of a nation "conceived in liberty" and a "government of the people, by the people, for the people," and still deny *habeas corpus* rights during the Civil War for such "crimes" as having a friend who was arrested for disloyalty or saying that the United States government was oppressive.[50] And they show up in a Woodrow Wilson who could fight a war "to see that liberty is made secure for mankind," while imprisoning a woman named Rose Pastor Stokes for ten years under the Espionage and Seditions Acts of 1917–18 for uttering the opinion that "I am for the people and the government is for the profiteers."[51] The detention of Japanese-Americans during World War II, the years of racial segregation and of McCarthyism are but better-known instances of a heritage of ambivalence.

And as the United States' global power grew, so did the number of people affected by that ambivalence. In the first years of the republic, with Europe an ocean and months of sailing away, the matter was not so urgent. George Washington could warn in his 1796 Farewell Address as president that the United States ought not entangle itself in "permanent [foreign] alliances;" Jefferson could echo him; John Quincy Adams could insist that the young nation "goes not abroad in search of monsters to destroy" and none would think them strange. But by the late nineteenth and early twentieth centuries, despite Henry Cabot Lodge's successful rearguard action against Woodrow Wilson's League of Nations, such isolationism sounded as anachronistic as a doctor who recommended treating dysentery with the bleeding of Washington's time or diarrhea with the laudanum of Adams's.

The question now was not *whether* we would "go abroad" but for what purpose and with what attitude toward those whom we would find there. As the United States became an imperial power in the late nineteenth century, the issue of who was among the sanctified and virtuous and hence eligible for full recognition of their rights became more complicated. No longer was it just domestic subjects, just the Native American, the dissenter, the woman or the slave (and her descendants) whose cases put the challenge to Americans. Now it was the globe at large. How would an exceptional nation see its role in relationship to what William Howard Taft, when serving as Governor of the Philippines, called "our little brown brothers"?

Congregational minister Josiah Strong's 1885 bestseller, *Our Country: Its Possible Future and Its Present Crisis*, a plea to impose America's Christian values on the world, presented a common view. "We are the chosen people," Strong averred. God was "not only preparing in our Anglo-Saxon civilization the die with which to stamp the people of the earth, but . . . also massing behind that die the mighty power with which to press it."[52] Here was the city set on the hill prepared in the name of freedom to levy its truth on those not "chosen," not worthy, whether they liked it or not. America's Manifest Destiny extended now well beyond the Pacific shores.

William McKinley fought the first foreign war, the Spanish-American, carried out in the name of human rights, as Warren Zimmerman points out in his masterly *First Great Triumph: How Five Americans Made Their Country a World Power*. U.S. intervention in Cuba was designed, in McKinley's words, "to put an end to the barbarities, bloodshed, starvation, and . . . miseries now existing there," but neither McKinley nor Teddy Roosevelt had any intention of allowing Cuba to set its destiny by itself, much less the Philippines, Hawaii, Guam, or Puerto Rico.[53] All of them were "liberated" in the name of freedom and then for a time at least (for some, a time not yet concluded) subject to American control. Vietnam and Latin America are contemporary examples of the syndrome: the city set on a hill seeks to establish a new world but ends up fostering repression and death at least in part because it cannot find the right balance between offering itself as a model and forcing that model on others who will not follow and because it is disinclined to honor the rights of those, like Communists, it finds unworthy.

• • •

That syndrome has not always had the upper hand, of course—witness two wars in Europe that left the continent far freer and, after the second at least, human rights more secure. Largely as a result of that second war, the recognition grew on Americans, even if often through a glass darkly, that if freedom and democracy *were* to be successfully exported, it would be a task not just for the United States but for everyone, and it would require recognition that human rights belong to human beings, whether we find them virtuous or not. The first American to put that clearly was Franklin Roosevelt, who insisted that his four freedoms—of speech and worship; from want and from fear—applied "everywhere in the world." His speech contained those words—"everywhere in the world"— several times. His advisor, Harry Hopkins, questioned the phrase. "That covers a lot of territory, Mr. President," he said, "I don't know how interested Americans are going to be in the people of Java." And Roosevelt replied, "I'm afraid they'll have to be some day, Harry. The world is getting so small that even the people in Java are getting to be our neighbors." That was in January 1941, less than a year before the beginning of a war in the Pacific that would prove the prescience of the president and less than five years before the U.N. would be established to help make his dream come true.[54]

The first person to translate that global vision into a universal compact was Eleanor Roosevelt and her colleagues who drafted the Universal Declaration of Human Rights (UDHR), adopted by the United Nations in 1948. The UDHR is the bedrock of all international human rights covenants. It has been accorded the status of "customary international law" by international bodies of jurisprudence around the world and been incorporated, at least in part, into dozens of national constitutions and legal statutes. It is in fact a far more revolutionary document than even its authors may have conceived. The U.S. State Department may well have sensed that when, at the time of the declaration's adoption, it emphasized that the document was to have no force of law but constituted only a "hortatory statement of aspirations." "Glittering generalities," anyone?

The declaration provides a set of norms or guidelines, "best practices," if you will, by which to recognize the dignity and autonomy of the individual, set limits to tyranny, and organize a decent society. It is, in other words, a blueprint for civilized behavior. For most of human history, the definition of what constituted "civilized behavior" was set by those who held the most power: military, political, economic. Until Great Britain, then the most dominant nation in the world, abolished slavery in its territories in 1833, to take but one example, that practice, while condemned by some, did not begin to assume the widespread mantle of ignominy it had garnered by the end of the nineteenth century.[55]

But allowing the powerful alone to be the arbiters of which behavior was acceptable and which was not had many serious drawbacks. Not surprisingly, the powerful tended to look with favor upon the status quo because that was what benefited *them*. Those on the margins of society—women, the poor, racial, religious, and sexual minorities—had very little say in creating the prevailing norms. When the powerful were also ruthless, as they so often were, building a "civilized" world could seem a very daunting task indeed.

It took the enormity of the Holocaust to fire the world's imagination into conceiving universal human rights. It was not that the concept of "rights" was new. The Magna Carta had spawned the notion in 1215 and several nations, including the United States with its Bill of Rights, adopted in 1791, had recognized that their own citizens could claim a set of rights. But it took the UDHR to institutionalize FDR's concept that rights applied "everywhere in the world," that *every* human being, merely by virtue of having been born a human, was entitled to the recognition and protection of her rights. You don't have to belong to a certain class or caste; you don't have to show proof of citizenship; and you don't even have to be a "good" person, at least when it comes to such fundamental rights as the right to life or not to be tortured. You just have to "show up." This was a revolutionary thought.

As was the way the Declaration was created and adopted. For it was created not by a tiny handful of the elite, the powerful; it was drafted by representatives from a wide variety of religious and cultural traditions; debated by every country that belonged to the U.N. in 1948; and voted on affirmatively by nations from every corner of the globe. It was, in other words, the expression of a shared commitment to a common vision of the world. And the dozens of human rights treaties, covenants, and conventions that have grown out of the UDHR are, too. This is one of the reasons why the charge that universal human rights are solely a Western phenomenon is so bogus. No matter what the philosophical origin of the rights prescribed in the Declaration, they now belonged to everybody. The UDHR itself has been translated into 365 different languages.

But this meant that the interpretation and enforcement of those rights belonged to everybody also, that the responsibility to define a righteous public life and make it come about was not just the task of *one* city set on a hill (or even one city and its political and cultural allies), but of all such "metropolises." And it meant that every one of those cities, including the most powerful and "exceptional," was subject to the same rules and the same judgment. For if the powerful showed no respect for the common vision, why should any other country? If the powerful did as they pleased, how could we defend human rights against the charge that they were merely one more mechanism by which the strong control the weak? If the powerful were oblivious to international human rights standards, why ought not the terrorists be, as well?

The UDHR asked for a monumental shift in thinking from the United States, to say nothing of its practice. It asked that the standards by which the balance was set between liberty and order be determined in some measure not just by American citizens (the elect) but by the international community (the inhabitants), that the social compact be extended beyond the borders of the country and that the country thereby recognizes, in theory if not in fact, some limits to sovereignty. It asked that virtue have no relation to rights, at least not the most important. It asked that decisions about enforcement of rights (and the use of force in general) be made in collaboration with others and pursued in accordance with agreed upon rules. It asked that the United States, now the most powerful country in the world, be a good world citizen, a responsible supporter of the international human rights regimen as manifested in human rights treaties, courts, and enforcement bodies. It asked that we be gracious in the exercise of our power, restrained in the propagation of our Truth, multilateral in our international relations, and cognizant that our own interests are usually maximized when the interests of others enter as much as possible into the calculus of our own.

Not surprisingly, these imperatives met with strong resistance from the very beginning. The impulse in the American character to restrict those who may create the social compact to the elect and worthy was far from spent. Senator John Bricker demanded shortly after the adoption of the UDHR that the United States withdraw from all U.N. human rights instruments because they were "completely foreign to American law and tradition."[56] Forty years later a spokesperson for Senator Jesse Helms, reflecting his boss's view, could say of all international human rights law, "It's an appalling intrusion by the UN . . . there's only one court that matters here. That's the U.S. Supreme Court. There's only one law that applies. That's the U.S. Constitution."[57]

Sometimes rejection by the United States of multilateralism and the human rights regimen has been robust. A cartoon popular during the Vietnam War era, more true to life than it was amusing, showed a much beribboned U.S. general talking on the phone to the president of some beleaguered country and saying, "Become a democracy by tomorrow or we bomb the shit out of you." Other times it has been more sophisticated but no less pointed. During the

2000 presidential campaign, Condoleeza Rice, now National Security Advisor, wrote that "Foreign policy in a Republican administration . . . will proceed from the firm ground of the national interest, not from the interests of an illusory international community,"[58] a sentiment that would come back to haunt her less than two years later as she and her President systematically sought the support of that "illusory" community for the war on terrorism.

And yet, despite the many hiccups along the way, a broad consensus across both Republican and Democratic administrations had emerged by the 2000 election that repudiated Senator Bricker's blanket condemnation of international human rights instruments (the United States has ratified, albeit with many reservations and much lassitude, five major human rights treaties and signed many more); recognized the legitimate role of bodies such as the United Nations Human Rights Commission; integrated advocacy for democracy and human rights into larger U.S. foreign policy stratagems; acknowledged that the violation of human rights in this country, be it the denial of civil rights to African Americans or the existence of poverty in the world's most affluent nation, had a deleterious effect on our interests overseas; rejected a rabid unilateralism that trampled on other nations' interests in the formulation of our own; affirmed that U.S. military power was best exercised within a context of international sanction (the Persian Gulf War, the Kosovo War); and saw clearly that diseases and the Internet know no national boundaries; that global markets make mincemeat of borders, and that security fails without friendships.

Moreover, such a vision reflected the opinion of the American people, 73 percent of whom told pollsters that they regarded themselves as citizens of the world, not just the United States, and 44 percent of whom agreed with that sentiment strongly.[59] Ironically, it was candidate George Bush who best caught the spirit of much of this bipartisan consensus when he reiterated over and over again in his campaign that "If we are an arrogant nation, [other countries] will view us that way, but if we're a humble nation, they'll respect us."

Wise words and especially so in a post-9/11 world, for it is exactly that sense of international solidarity fostered by American "humility," that mutual commitment to human rights norms and standards, that the Al Qaeda operatives seek to undermine. For if they can convince large numbers of people that the values of democracy and respect for the rule of law in the name of which the war against terrorism is ostensibly being fought are a mere chimera, a ruse, a means to impose Western interests on the rest of the world; if they can taint the credibility of the U.N. and other international institutions, if they can strip the international order of its legitimacy by labeling its greatest champion, the United States, a hypocrite, a religious bigot and a tyrant, they will have taken a major step toward discrediting international human rights norms themselves and justifying the ascendancy of their own.

One would think, therefore, that the United States would have every interest, especially now, in safeguarding human rights both at home and around the globe. Yet since September 11, 2001 that part of the American disposition inclined to trump liberty with order, to engage in moral preening, to reserve rights for the worthy and Right to the powerful, has emerged with a vengeance.

Has it all been a matter of fear? Did 9/11, as we have heard so often, "change everything"? Or is the truth more insidious?

Universal human rights rest on a very fragile scaffolding. They are different from rights that are guaranteed in the constitutions of sovereign states. If my right as a U.S. citizen to vote or to exercise free speech is violated, I can go to court and, at least theoretically, have that violation remedied. The executive branch of government is required to enforce the ruling of the court, by force if ultimately necessary.

International human rights are different. There *are* international laws governing human rights and international courts to interpret them. But there is no executive, no sheriff, no police officer, and no soldier whose job it is in any consistent fashion to enforce those laws or the findings of those courts. The international community has conveniently arranged it so that human rights rest largely on voluntary compliance supplemented by public opprobrium, private diplomacy, support for international legal structures, occasional economic sanctions, and the rare military intervention. For these mechanisms to work, for human rights claims to be of any consequence, the nations of the world, and especially the most powerful and influential, must show them their fealty.

Many of the most influential players in the Bush administration would regard themselves as champions of human rights. But the role they envision for the United States in the world and the ways they have skewered human rights at home undermine the very premises of the human rights revolution. For some, that was a goal nurtured long before September 11. The attack on the United States merely provided the opportunity (and a golden one it was) to do what they had always wanted to do: to send the human rights scaffolding, like the towers, plunging to the ground.

• • •

The Monastery of the Empty Moon has no gate. The Chief Priest was once asked how the monastery protected itself against thieves. "There is nothing here to steal," he said. "We give everything away." "But what of troublesome people?" he was asked. "We ignore them," said the priest. "Does that work?" asked his interlocutor. The Chief Priest covered his ears, closed his eyes and refused to answer. Finally his questioner left in disgust. "It *does* work," the Chief Priest called after him.

The foreign policy mandarins whose views have shaped the American response to the threat of terrorism would have no truck with the Chief Priest's faith in the power of passivity. They are no isolationists, no Pat Buchanans insisting that the "best way to avoid any attack on our nation or its armed forces is . . . by disengaging the United States from ideological, religious, ethnic, historic, or territorial quarrels that are none of America's business." They are no avatars of the libertarian Cato Institute declaring that "the best defense is to give no offense."[60]

On the contrary. Candidate Bush may have disparaged "nation-building" and observed that "Our nation should be slow to engage troops. . . . We can never again ask the military to fight a political war." Rice may have declared during the campaign her opposition to "using the American armed forces as the world's '911' . . . [because it will] fuel concerns . . . that the United States has decided to enforce notions of 'limited sovereignty.'" But *President* Bush brought into office with him a coterie of policy makers, starting with his vice president, Dick Cheney, determined to remake the world and remake it in America's image.[61]

Such missionary zeal, as we have seen, has deep roots in the American experience. In contemporary terms, it goes back at least to John Foster Dulles, secretary of state (1953–59) under President Dwight D. Eisenhower, who brought the fervor of his Christian convictions into the Cold War struggle against "godless" Communism. But whereas Dulles, despite his bellicose threats to roll back the Iron Curtain, had been content to "contain" Communism, the new missionaries want to leave an American imprint on all that surrounds us—to, quite literally, dominate the world. To do that, these neoconservatives reason, the United States has to exploit fully the one resource that no other country or combination of countries can possibly match: our enormous military might.

Beginning in 1992 when he was secretary of defense under the first President Bush, Vice President Cheney has been a key patron of a series of policy papers that lay out a plan to force the world to conform to America's bidding. First made public in the

Defense Department's *Defense Strategy for the 1990s*, published in 1993, just as Cheney completed his service as secretary of defense under the first President Bush, the plan sought to take advantage of the collapse of the Soviet Union to assert U.S. hegemony. The point, as Colin Powell, then chairman of the Joint Chiefs of Staff, put it to Congress in 1992 in describing an earlier incarnation of the plan, was to build up such military power that no other nation on earth would ever dare to challenge us. "I want to be the bully on the block," Powell said, utilizing a telling, if perhaps unfortunate, metaphor.[62]

With Cheney and his cohort out of office, the task of promoting American preeminence fell to the neoconservative consortium, Project for a New American Century (PNAC), founded in 1997 by William Kristol and Robert Kagan of the right-wing magazine, *The Weekly Standard*. In its 1997 "Statement of Principles," PNAC made clear that its name meant exactly what it said: the twenty-first century was to be the "new *American* century," and the only way to make that happen was through massive military power. "A Reaganite policy of military strength and moral clarity . . . is necessary," the statement read, "if the U.S. is to . . . ensure our security and greatness in [the coming century]." The signers of the "Statement of Principles," in addition to Cheney, included Jeb Bush, the president's brother; Donald Rumsfeld, now secretary of defense; Paul Wolfowitz, now assistant secretary of defense; I. Lewis Libby, now chief of staff and national security advisor to the vice president; Elliott Abrams, now senior director of the national security council; Paula Dobriansky, now under secretary of state for global affairs; and Zalmay Halilzad, now special envoy to Afghanistan. [63]

But exactly how was such "greatness" to be achieved? In 2000 PNAC came up with the answer in the form of a policy paper entitled *Rebuilding America's Defense: Strategies, Forces and Resources for a New Century*. Among its recommendations were that the United States undertake a massive increase in defense spending, the development of "a new family of nuclear weapons," permanent "constabulary missions" around the world led by the United States instead of the U.N., control of outer space and cyberspace, a permanent military presence in the Middle East and Southeast Asia, the creation of a U.S. Air Force "global first-strike force," and consideration of the removal from power of regimes in Iran, Iraq, and North Korea, which President Bush would dub two years later the "Axis of Evil." The ultimate goal was to do whatever it took to secure "unquestioned United States military preeminence," a *Pax Americana*, and to prevent any other country from ever challenging the United States, just as Cheney and Powell had outlined eight years before.[64] Like many similar policy tomes, *Rebuilding* laid out an ambitious program. But unlike most of the rest of them, this was an agenda that was actually to spring off the printed page and into life.

Its formal birth occurred on September 19, 2002, when the Bush administration, with Cheney et al. back in power, issued, as required by law, a summary of U.S. defense policy in the form of a document called *The National Security Strategy of the United States of America (NSS)*. While now official government policy and hence a much sanitized version of the privately authored *Rebuilding*, *NSS* left no doubt that "our best defense is a good offense," that the United States "will not hesitate to act alone, if necessary" against terrorists and that "the greater the threat, . . . the more compelling the case for anticipatory [preemptive] action to defend ourselves, even if uncertainty remains as to the time and place of the enemy's attack." The document, in parallel to *Rebuilding*, made reference to military bases "beyond Western Europe and Northeast Asia," the development of "long range precision strike capabilities," and the need to protect U.S. interests in outer space. Not surprisingly, North Korea and Iraq (though not Iran, which was in the midst of an internal struggle to open up its political system) were singled out as "rogue states" that, among other things, "display no regard for international law"—a criticism tinged with irony given that the NSS reserved some of its most vituperative language for an attack on the International Criminal Court (ICC). "In exercising our leadership," the report concluded, "we will respect the values, judgments, and interests of our friends and partners. Still, we will be prepared to act apart when our interests and unique responsibilities require."[65] In the NSS, the bully inside *Defense Strategy for the 1990s* and *Rebuilding* had been told to behave himself, to dress up, comb his hair, clean his teeth, but, despite the cosmetics, his inner nature kept threatening to break through.

For one thing, his sponsors kept giving the truth away. "What should [the U.S.'s international] role be?" Kristol and Kagan had asked. And they had answered, "Benevolent global hegemony." "Having defeated the 'evil empire,' the United States enjoys strategic and ideological predominance. The first objective of US foreign policy should be to preserve and enhance that predominance. . . ."[66] Though the NSS made gestures toward multilateralism, the second Bush Administration (in marked contrast to the first with its coalition-based "New World Order") had signaled its contempt for the "values, judgments, and interests of our friends and partners" almost from its inception—with its rejection of the Kyoto Protocol on global warming and withdrawal from the Antiballistic Missile Treaty; its "unsigning" of the International Criminal Court and threats to stop all funding of U.N. peacekeeping missions; its veto of a protocol designed to put teeth into the Biological Weapons Convention; its vote against the optional protocol to the U.N. Convention Against Torture; its review of the U.S. commitment to cease using antipersonnel landmines by 2006 and its solitary refusal to accept any norms related to civilian possession of small arms in the U.N. convention to limit small weapons. These actions, coupled with the imposition of high protective tariffs on steel imports, the increase in government farm subsidies, the unilateral action against Iraq in the face of Security Council opposition, and Secretary Rumsfeld's regular assertion that the war against terrorism "should not be fought by committee," stripped the Bush Administration of its multilateral veneer.[67]

But *not*, paradoxically enough, of all justification for claiming a commitment to human rights. For though, as we have seen, the sacrifice of multilateralism is in and of itself a major blow to the human rights scaffolding, many of the Bush unilateralists are no George Kennans, declaring, "I would like to see our government gradually withdraw from its public advocacy of democracy and human rights . . . I don't think any such questions should enter into our diplomatic relations with other countries. . . . The State Department [and] the White House . . . have more important things to do."[68] They are no Henry Kissingers confiding to Augusto Pinochet's foreign minister, "I hold the strong view that human rights is not appropriate for discussion in a foreign policy context."[69]

No, the situation with the Bush strategists is much more complicated than that and has thrown some human rights advocates off stride. The PNAC's "Statement of Principles," after all, called for "A Reaganite policy of military strength *and moral clarity*" [emphasis added] Kristol and Kagan have often editorialized about the importance of grounding U.S. foreign policy in moral principles and insisted that "No one today can doubt that support for democracy [is] profoundly in our strategic interest."[70] Elliott Abrams has written that "preserving [U.S.] dominance will not only advance our national interests but will preserve peace and promote the cause of democracy and human rights."[71] Paul Wolfowitz, much of whose father's family perished in the Holocaust, has made a similar point: "The greatest advantage the United States had over the Soviet Union during the Cold War was our moral advantage," he has said, and "It's a mistake to dismiss [human rights] concern as merely humanitarian and not related to real interests."[72] Wolfowitz strongly favored U.S. military intervention to stop genocide in Bosnia. The *NSS* itself proclaims that "We will champion the cause of human dignity and oppose those who resist it." And the war in Iraq was ostensibly fought in part to put an end to Saddam Hussein's outrageous human rights record.

The problem is not that these neoconservatives think the world would be better off with less democracy or fewer regimes that respect human rights. The problem is that they have a very narrow, ideological understanding of human rights and would impose that understanding on the rest of the world. ("Become a democracy by tomorrow or we bomb the shit out of you.") The problem is that they display enormous contempt for the international instrumentalities that are designed to give weight to human rights claims. And the problem is that they have a raging aversion to having those claims applied to the United States.

President Bush's speech to the graduating class at West Point in June 2002 put that narrow understanding of human rights dramatically on display. "The twentieth century," he said, "ended with a single surviving model of human progress, based on the non-negotiable demands of human dignity, the rule of law, limits on the power of the state, respect for women and private property and free speech and equal justice and religious tolerance . . . In our development aid, in our diplomatic efforts, in our international broadcasting, and in our educational assistance, the United States will promote moderation and tolerance and human rights." Words similar to these had appeared in the January 2002 State of the Union address and would subsequently appear in the *NSS* and in an editorial the president wrote to commemorate the first anniversary of 9/11. They are good words, if fairly vague ones, promising words, even eloquent. But notice what the president *didn't* say.

"In our development aid . . . , diplomatic efforts . . . , international broadcasting and . . . educational assistance, the United States will promote . . . human rights," he said. But what about in our military policies, in our relations with our allies, in our interpretation of national sovereignty, in our recognition of the rights of foreign nationals, in our support for international institutions, in our ratification of international human rights treaties, in our interrogation of prisoners, in our treatment of those who threaten us, in our conduct of the war on terror? It is in these respects that the human rights rubber hits the national security road, and it is in these respects that the United States has failed so miserably.

Partly that is because we have interpreted human rights through an American lens, projected what they mean on the world stage through the gauze of our own constitution and historical experience. "America's constitution has served us well," says the *NSS*. "Many other nations . . . have successfully incorporated [its] core principles into their own systems of governance. History has not been kind to those nations which ignored or flouted the rights and aspirations of their people." Here the "rights and aspirations" of the world's people are explicitly identified with the "core principles" of the U.S. Constitution—principles such as those the president pointed to at West Point: free speech, religious tolerance, respect for private property. But admirable as these principles may be, they hardly exhaust the lexicon of human rights. For the U.S. Constitution displays a host of lacunae when it comes to universal human rights: it does not codify social and economic rights, for example; it does not recognize the cogency of international law; it does not, at least as currently interpreted, preclude the use of the death penalty or even the execution of juvenile offenders, though the United States is the last remaining country in the world to tolerate that practice.

By making the American understanding of rights the plumb line for all others, we deprive human rights of the credibility they derive from their transnational character. For it is, after all, the *universality* of human rights that lends them their moral power.

Kristol and Kagan yearn for "moral clarity" in the pursuit of U.S. foreign policy but, absent a broad if imperfect international consensus, moral clarity is largely in the eye of the beholder. I am reminded that when a group of Polish children were brought to Auschwitz after being caught stealing coal, they were housed with the adults because there were no separate facilities for children. The Nazis were perturbed by the thought of children sleeping in the company of adult men. Might something untoward happen to them? So the children were given lethal injections in order that the "morals" of the camp might be preserved. Moral distinctions often fall peril to the biases of those who make them. That is the danger of predicating rights on the virtue of those who claim them, a danger, as we have seen, that Americans have succumbed to frequently throughout our history and to which we are especially prone right now: whomever the powerful dub an "evildoer," so may his rights be suspended or ignored.

But when it comes to human rights, the rules are usually clear—established by international law, interpreted by international courts. Human rights are not dependent upon one country's history, constitution, whim, or might. They are not contingent on their claimants' "goodness." This is exactly what makes the most fundamental of them "nonnegotiable," in the president's words. Not, as one suspects he means, because they carry the force of an American stick behind them, but because they have won the assent—largely the voluntary assent—of millions of people around the globe.

How could the partisans of American preeminence *not* be uncomfortable with that? For if human rights are not grounded solely in an American ethos, if they derive their power from the approbation they receive from the United Nations, international courts, nongovernmental organizations, and dozens of other countries around the world, then all people, "everywhere in the world," may claim them, not just those of whom we approve. Then national security may trump them only with the imprimatur of a larger authority than that of one nation alone, even if it be an "exceptional" one. Then they apply to us as well as everyone else. Then there may actually be some limits to national sovereignty.

In this light, it is easy to see why Rice was so eager to dub the international community an "illusion," easy to see why the proponents of a new American century are so intent upon defining and enforcing human rights in such narrow terms: in order that they might get ahead of the curve, so to speak, and obviate the inexorable march—from the passage of the UDHR in 1948 . . . to the worldwide ratification of one human rights treaty after another . . . to the proliferation of indigenous human rights groups in virtually every country in the world . . . to the decision by the European Union that national laws would be subject to international review . . . to the establishment of war crimes tribunals for the former Yugoslavia and Rwanda . . . to the decision of the British courts regarding Augusto Pinochet . . . to the ratification of the International Criminal Court—the inexorable march toward the preeminence not of one country's preferences alone but of a culture of respect for human rights that transcends any one nation's predilections. *Such a vision must, very simply, be destroyed. And if it can be destroyed in the very name of human rights, so much the better.* So much more perfect the symmetry. So much more clever the irony.

So a novice president (or perhaps, more accurately, that novice president's calculating coterie), confronted with the enormity of 9/11, seized the moment to crusade—to crusade against "evildoers" everywhere in the name of freedom, the "rule of law," "human rights," and "our very way of life." This was no "city set on a hill," the eyes of all people to be upon it that "men shall say of succeeding plantations, 'Lord, make it like that of New England.'" Nothing as passive as that. No, this was a "chosen people . . . preparing . . . the die with which to stamp the people of the earth

[and] . . . massing behind that die the mighty powers with which to press it." Of the other 190 countries in the world, Vice President Cheney asked starkly a few days after 9/11, "Are they going to stand with the United States and believe in freedom and democracy and civilization or are they going to stand with the terrorists and the barbarians?"[73]

How profound the paradox. A Republican president who promised to restore humility to U.S. foreign policy revealing, as he said at the National Cathedral on September 14, 2001 that "our responsibility to history is . . . clear: to . . . rid the world of evil." Even Ronald Reagan had limited the evil with which he was determined to do away to a single empire. Not since Democrat Woodrow Wilson had a U.S. president taken on such a grandiose ideal: "Nothing less depends on this decision [ratification of the League of Nations]," Wilson had said in the last speech he ever gave, " . . . than the liberation and salvation of the world."[74] But how profound the paradox. A Wilsonian president utilizing not Wilson's appeal to international partnership to save the world but the no-holds-barred war throttle of an Andrew Jackson. "Jacksonians," says the historian Walter Russell Mead, "often figure . . . as the least likely to support Wilsonian initiatives for a better world." But then he goes on to describe the Jacksonian spirit in foreign policy:

> One in which honor . . . and faith in military institutions play a [great] role. . . . At a very basic level, a feeling of kinship exists among Americans: we have one set of rules for dealing with each other and a very different set for the outside world. . . . The United States must be vigilant and strongly armed. Our diplomacy must be cunning, forceful, and no more scrupulous than anybody else's. There is absolutely nothing wrong with subverting foreign governments or assassinating foreign leaders. Thus, Jacksonians are more likely to tax political leaders with a failure

> to employ vigorous measures than to worry about the niceties of
> international law. . . . Jacksonians believe that there is an honor
> code in international life . . . and those who live by the code will
> be treated under it. But those who violate the code—who com-
> mit terrorist acts in peacetime, for example—forfeit its protec-
> tion and deserve no consideration.[75]

George Bush is that astonishing rarity: a Wilsonian in Jacksonian
breeches. And how profound the paradox. A conservative
Jacksonian president, whose basic political philosophy, like that of
all true conservatives, is to be suspicious of excessive government
because they know how easily human beings can be corrupted by
power, presiding over a government that threatens to extend its
reach into every corner of the globe and every quiet alcove of
American domestic life.

Paradoxical, yes. But up against the many glad qualities of the
American experiment, these darker sentiments have, as we have
seen, been here all along. In the righteousness of the Pilgrim. In
the insistence on ours as an exceptional nation. In the inclination
to allow order to subvert liberty. In the demand for virtue as a pre-
requisite for rights. In the temptation to extend an empire. In the
suspicion of global institutions. In the urge to economically rule
the world.

To their credit, the Bush partisans have, as we have also seen,
rarely made a secret of their endgame or their methods. The strategic groundwork for a crusading America intent upon casting aside
international constraints and remaking the world in its image was
laid as far back as the 1970s when the conservative think tank, the
American Enterprise Institute (AEI), convinced of the redemptive
mission of the United States, began calling for American hegemony.
It was given intellectual heft by Harvard's neoconservative political
theorist, Samuel Huntington, with his contention that the West

faces a "clash of civilizations" between itself and Islam.[76] It has been repeatedly bolstered by the dyspeptic writings of former AEI Vice President John Bolton, now under Secretary of State for Arms Control and International Security, who has spent a career debunking the U.N. and anything else that "inhibits America's ability . . . to use force" and who, recognizing that support for human rights means sacrificing an element of sovereignty, has ridiculed their importance, saying they include "values often at war with liberty."[77]

Nor have those who would undermine human rights at the domestic level come to their perspectives suddenly. Attorney General John Ashcroft hardly required 9/11 to convince him that "a calculated, malignant, devastating evil has arisen in our world," for he had predicted in a 1999 speech at Bob Jones University that any culture that had any king other than Jesus would "release Barabbas—criminality, destruction, thievery, the lowest and the least."[78] When he was in Congress, Ashcroft favored legislation (the Effective Death Penalty and Antiterrorism Act of 1996) that put severe limitations on the right of *habeas corpus,* limitations he has subsequently applied in the treatment of so-called "unlawful combatants," whether U.S. citizens or not.

Those in the current American government, then, who, no matter their rhetoric, are heirs to that portion of the American experience which, if allowed to flourish, would bring down the human rights scaffolding are at the moment robust and regnant, their city gleaming, their hubris undimmed. But they have forgotten just one thing: that if, according to Winthrop, the city set on a hill *failed* to be decent and humane, if it "shall open the mouths of enemies to speak evil of the ways of God," then prayers shall turn into curses and "we shall surely perish out of the good land whither we pass over this vast sea. . . ."[79]

The Founders of the country recognized this, too. For it was not only the people who retained their rights by virtue of their worthiness but the government that retained its legitimacy by virtue of its benevolence. What was the moral principle that underlay the authority of government? Not fear, for fear was the principle of a despot. Samuel Adams put it this way: "We may look up to Armies for our Defence," he reminded James Warren, "but Virtue is our best security. It is not possible that any State should long remain free, where Virtue is not supremely honored."[80] And what applies to a government's treatment of its own citizens applies as well to its treatment of the world.

Empires may be born by force but they are not long sustained by it. They are sustained by a capacity to peddle a better idea than one's adversaries and to practice what you preach, to resolve conflicts equitably, to be such a generous friend, such an honorable guest, that your host and hostess are eager for your company. We knew that during the cold war. We knew we needed friends; we knew we had a better idea—democracy, freedom, human rights and respect for the rule of law. Debate as we will whether the United States today seeks empire and whether, if it does, that quest be just, what is beyond dispute is that we have forgotten what for so long we knew. Moralism mixed with hubris driven by repression and force leads to resentment, resistance, and rebellion.

This is no way to way to fight a war on terrorism. For it paints us in threatening terms, not sympathetic ones; hypocritical hues, not honorable colors. It alienates our friends whose help we need. It makes it impossible for moderate Muslims to argue our case without appearing to be doing the bidding of the bully. It casts us as a global policeman who cares nothing about the law. It implicates us in the hypocrisy of regarding others' sovereignty as limited while holding inviolate our own. It rewards bin Laden's rant against "the iniquitous United Nations" by our, too, neutering that body. It makes the "clash of civilizations" a self-fulfilling prophecy and the quest for common values a hollow one.

And it leads to the delusion that the antagonism we experience is not about our policies and practices but about who we are, about our ideals, what we stand for, and our very existence.[81] Not only does such self-delusion provide the perfect excuse not to subject those policies to scrutiny, but it also forces us to fight the war on terrorism under the gravest handicap, with one hand tied behind our back. For what we stand for, at our best, is our greatest strength. What we stand for is the "unalienable right" of every person to pursue "life, liberty, and . . . happiness." What we stand for is equal justice and equal opportunity for all, free speech, a free press, fair elections, and no fear that secret police will storm your house at night because you have criticized the government. What we stand for is the highest of respect for human rights, not the denial of legal counsel to suspects or the infliction of torture on prisoners.

These principles sound like clichés to Americans because we so take them for granted, but none of us can take them for granted anymore. And they are anything but clichés to the millions of people around the world who live every day with a very different reality. For such people, the United States has been a symbol of the best the world has to offer. "I respect the United States," said Hamda el-Mari, a twenty-two-year-old from the United Arab Emirates. "People in the United States have rights. In my country, we can't have rights. I would like to vote."[82] Our political and economic systems, for all their flaws, offer that better idea, that alternative ideology, that the retinue needs if it is to reject the dead-end blandishments of Al Qaeda.

If we fail to see that, if we allow ourselves to be convinced that it is our ideals, not our actions, that are under assault, that, despite our enormous power, our very "civilization" is at stake, then there are no limits to what we may do to defend ourselves and no limits on our allies, either. But if we take that route, we risk sacrificing those very ideals that most inspire the rest of the world; we risk suborning the conclusion that human rights are a mere bagatelle compared to life itself and that "all is fair . . . in war"—particularly a war of unlimited duration designed to "rid the world of evil."

Do that and we will have lost the war on terrorism for certain. For if we jettison the human rights scaffolding, we throw away the very measures of a good society. And without those, whatever victory we may obtain will surely be a Pyrrhic one.

CHAPTER 3

The Haunting of America (I):

How Countenancing Human Rights
Violations Overseas Does Us
Damage Here At Home

*The greatest evils have always found their way into
the life of men under the semblance of good.*[83]

Erasmus

He wore a firefighter's coat, and a respirator hung around his
neck. But, unlike other firefighters rushing toward the World Trade
Center on September 11, 2001 Shahram Hashemi had no helmet or
boots. That is because he was in fact not a professional firefighter
but a college student from Iran, on his way to his job as an intern at
the Bank of New York on Wall Street when the first tower collapsed.
Seeing several women, dazed and covered in ash, he guided them
into the lobby of the bank.

Thousands of people were running away from the blast, but some
people, firefighters and police, were heading toward it. "They knew
it might be the end of their lives," he said later, "but they went."
That inspired Hashemi to join them, to try to help. Racing in the
direction of the towers, he was soon in danger from the raging

flames. Near Battery Park, a firefighter spotted him and handed him a protective fireman's jacket. "Is there anything I can do?" Hashemi cried out. "Yes," the fireman shouted back. "We lost a lot of people back there." "It was a moment I will never forget," Hashemi recalled. "It was dark and fire was everywhere. You couldn't breathe. We knew that at any moment we could die. So I told the fireman, 'My name is Shahram Hashemi and just in case anything happens to me, let my family know.'" The fireman said he would, embraced the young Muslim, and then made the sign of the cross. "Christ protect you," he said.

Then Hashemi went to work, joining other civilians in teams, a volunteer fire brigade, sent to Ground Zero to fight the fires and look for survivors. Later he would carry water in buckets to the professionals who were struggling with the enormous blaze. Several times he came close to being killed and finally, when the forty-seven-story building at number seven collapsed, he became trapped inside, disoriented. Eventually he was spotted by a mobile triage unit and evacuated by ferry to a hospital. The doctors in the triage unit were all Jewish, Hashemi noted, perhaps from Beth Israel Hospital. And when the ordeal was finally over, he took time to reflect: "The way I see it," he said, "I was blessed by three religions that day. It was my Islamic faith that motivated me to go back and help. I was blessed in the name of Jesus at the most dangerous moment of my life, and then I was helped by Jewish doctors."[84]

Hashemi is a young man of enormous idealism and courage. The founder of the first Amnesty International student chapter at LaGuardia Community College and, more recently, at Adelphi University, he is convinced that what binds humanity together across religious and political divides is the claim we all can make to universal human rights. But there is one thing Shahram Hashemi may not have reckoned on: that, witness though he was to a terrible human rights calamity, it was not just the hijackers who would be its perpetrators.

• • •

The ambivalence about human rights that has long characterized Americans and their policy makers, as described in the last chapter, came back to haunt us on September 11. This is in no way to excuse or explain away the actions of the hijackers. In the weeks following the attacks, it was commonplace, particularly among some segments of the political left, to claim that the United States had brought the disaster on itself. Such a blame-the-victim mentality does disservice not only to those who perished on that day and whose legacy is an unblemished one but to the bedrock principle that underlies human rights in the first place: the notion that all blood flows red and its innocent spilling always a tragedy.

What the events of 9/11 taught us, however, is that there can indeed be enormous costs associated with committing or countenancing human rights crimes. Nowhere was that more true than in Afghanistan, the place that became the focus of the first phase of the war on terrorism, and Iraq, the venue for the second.

Eager to draw the Soviets into their own "Vietnam War," the United States began in 1979 supplying Islamic fundamentalists based in Pakistan with small-scale assistance to encourage their insurgency against the Communist-backed government in Kabul. "We didn't push the Russians to intervene," Zbigniew Brzezinski, then national security advisor to President Jimmy Carter, said later, "but we knowingly increased the probability that they would."[85] Over the next ten years, the Americans would provide $3 billion worth of military assistance, including Stinger missiles, to rebel forces. Among those receiving aid were a faction called Harakat-I-Inquilab-I-Islami, out of which the Taliban would eventually arise.

A case can be made that the United States bore at least a measure of responsibility, along with the Soviets, for the chaos that
ensued following the war and that eventually led to the rise of the
Taliban and their harboring of bin Laden.[86] There is no question
that, with the withdrawal of the Russians in 1989, many of the
Mujahedeen who had fought the occupation with the United States'
support, went on to commit widespread atrocities, including a massive number of rapes of children and women that paved the way for
Taliban rule.[87] Some critics have even claimed that the United
States, which initially hailed the Taliban as principled reformers
when they came to power in 1996, had facilitated their rise both as
a check on Iran and with the expectation that Afghanistan would
become a friendly avenue through which to ship oil and gas
extracted from Central Asia.

Tangled as the history is here and unreliable as hindsight can
be, what is beyond dispute is that throughout this period, the
United States aligned itself with a cast of unsavory characters,
including Pakistani dictator General Zia ul-Haq, whose fearsome
intelligence services were used to convey U.S. assistance to the
mujahideen. General Zia used the promotion of radical Islam with
its strict *shari'a* law to suppress democracy and human rights in
Pakistan. It therefore served his purpose to sponsor Islamic
extremists who, when their Soviet nemesis was vanquished, would
turn rabidly anti-American and provide Al Qaeda with both shock
troops and a home.[88]

It is impossible to say whether the choice of those radicals over
the Communists as the lesser of two evils was a wise one at the time
and whether the Islamists would have driven the Russians out of
Afghanistan even without U.S. aid. But, had greater weight been
given to human rights, including by the "human rights president,"
Jimmy Carter, the United States might at least have thought twice
about the potential consequences of its policy. Among those

consequences: the vast network of fundamentalist Islamic schools in Pakistan established by General Zia, many of which today supply sympathizers, if not soldiers, to Al Qaeda; and the large number of forts in mountain caves near Tora Bora erected with American assistance by the Afghan rebels during the civil war—the Soviets called them "the last word in NATO engineering"—that shielded bin Laden and many of his operatives during the 2001 U.S. military siege and may have aided in his escape.[89]

Moreover, there is a lingering sense in Pakistan in particular that the United States has betrayed its most fundamental values in the past (cozying up to dictators; ignoring the brutality of its allies) when it has appeared to suit its short-term interests, and there is no reason to think it will not do so again. Indeed, many Pakistanis feel that since the beginning of the war on terrorism, the United States has reverted to its past practice of subsuming others' interests to the transient interests of its own—by failing to make resolution of the dispute with India over Kashmir a priority; by refusing to call President Pervez Musharraf to account for his assumption of authoritarian powers; and by maintaining strict limits on American imports of Pakistani textiles in order to protect the U.S. textile industry. "America is like poison to me," one Pakistani clothing worker said recently. "I'm still bitter about it. I felt they were our friends." This is not an outlook the United States wants to foster in the world's second largest Muslim country.

• • •

Saddam Hussein did not suddenly go off his rocker when he invaded Kuwait in 1991. The United States knew long before then that Saddam was responsible for practices that would justify his reputation as a madman. We knew that, shortly after he became President of Iraq in 1979, he had videotaped a session of his party congress at which he personally ordered several members executed on the spot for "thinking" about plotting against him.[91] We knew that torture was commonplace in the country.[92] We knew, according to the 1984 State Department human rights report, that "Execution has been an established method for dealing with perceived political and military opponents of the [Iraqi] government."[93] We knew that Iraq had used chemical weapons during its war against Iran and that in 1987–88 such weapons killed over 100,000 Iraqi Kurds.

Yet, despite this knowledge, the United States not only failed to enter strenuous objection to Iraqi abuses (the Reagan administration offered only the most token protest about the massacre of the Kurds, for example, and opposed legislation that would have introduced stiff sanctions against Iraq);[94] it in fact had provided Saddam military and security assistance throughout the 1980s to carry on his war against Iran. This assistance included satellite photos, a computerized database to track political opponents, helicopters, video surveillance cameras, chemical analysis equipment, and numerous shipments of "bacteria/fungi/protozoa." A 1994 Senate Banking Committee investigation discovered that the United States had shipped dozens of biological agents, including strains of anthrax, to Iraq in the mid–1980s.[95] It has been reported that between 1980 and 1991, twenty-four U.S. companies supplied Iraq with weapons-related material; that the U.S. Department of Energy delivered essential nonfissile parts for Baghdad's nuclear weapons program; and that Iraqi military and armaments experts were trained in the United States.[96] After the Persian Gulf War was over, the Pentagon documented evidence of war crimes, including the use of acid baths and electric drills on prisoners, with an eye toward prosecution, but high officials in the first Bush administration scotched the project.

The United States did not "make" Saddam Hussein. But had his human rights record been more of a factor in our policy decisions, we might well have taken steps to curb his appetite for threatening behavior before it led to war. At the very least we might have resisted supplying him with the tools to do his dirty work. As it was, the comment Saddam's cousin, Ali Hassan al-Majid (known as "Chemical Ali") was overheard to have made with reference to the gassing of the Kurds, was entirely understandable: "Who is going to say anything [about our actions]?" Ali Hassan asked. "The international community? Fuck them!"[97]

• • •

If the threats to world order posed by the Taliban's Afghanistan and Saddam Hussein's Iraq were in part facilitated by the suborning of human rights violations, so, too, did such sufferance nourish the soil out of which the hijackers themselves emerged in Egypt and Saudi Arabia.

Islamic fundamentalists in Egypt have frequently displayed a penchant for violence, as the novelist Naguib Mahfouz learned when he was viciously attacked and maimed for life in 1994 after he supported peace with Israel and denounced the *fatwa* calling for the death of Salman Rushdie. Who can forget the 1999 attack on tourists in Luxor that killed fifty-eight? Measures to protect against such wanton slaughter are not only legitimate but essential. Far too often, however, in the name of providing security, Egyptian authorities have overreached. They have targeted those affiliated with groups like the Muslim Brotherhood, which has been associated with terrorism, whether or not the individuals have been accused of committing or advocating violence themselves. Given the Brotherhood's political popularity (it often supplies economic support to the poor who have been overlooked by government programs), these arrests may well be designed to prevent the defendants from running for office or organizing politically.

Even more disturbingly, Egyptian law exerts tight control over the press and prohibits strikes, public meetings, and election rallies. Trade unionists protesting issues of worker safety and activists criticizing the medical services offered by a state-owned company, among many others, have been harassed or imprisoned for their efforts.[98] In such an environment, only those who parrot the government line can feel entirely safe.

Saad Eddin Ibrahim dared to stray from that line. A highly respected professor of sociology, outspoken advocate of democracy, and head of Egypt's Ibn Khaldun Center for Development, Ibrahim, who holds dual United States and Egyptian citizenship, has been a persistent critic of radical Islamists, but it was not Islamists who would cost him his freedom. It was the Egyptian government that closed down his center and sentenced him to prison for seven years after he criticized corruption, election irregularities, and the treatment of minorities by the Egyptian state. Ibrahim was eventually released in late 2002, but the message had been sent to all those would-be moderate voices in Egypt: speak up and this, too, may happen to you.

One of the factors in Ibrahim's release may have been a threat by President Bush, who recognized how damaging the case was to the reputation of one of our staunchest allies, to withhold additional military assistance to Egypt. This was a marked departure from past administrations' coddling of the Mubarak regime and overlooking its human rights record. But Bush's action failed to win the United States many friends in Egypt. For after turning a blind eye for years to the political repression fostered by the second largest recipient of its military aid, the United States' sudden interest in the Ibrahim case sparked widespread cynicism. Was it only the professor's American citizenship that had prompted the president to act? Why had the United States never shown a similar level of concern for other Egyptians?

With no free elections, no other means of expressing dissent, and little sense that Western powers care about their government's treatment of its critics, it is no surprise that some Egyptians find the ideology of the Islamic militants appealing. Despite years of pulling its punches about Egypt's human rights violations, the United States has found itself with few defenders in its struggle with Al Qaeda, much less its war in Iraq. Exactly what, one wonders, had our years of "solicitude" gotten us?

• • •

The case of Saudi Arabia is not that different. Article 39 of the Saudi constitution bans anything that may give rise to "mischief and discord." "Witchcraft," "black magic," and "corruption on earth" are also against the law in Saudi Arabia, and those convicted of them can receive sentences as severe as 1,000 lashes, amputation of limbs, or even death by beheading. But what exactly constitutes mischief, discord, witchcraft, black magic, and corruption on earth is almost impossible to say ahead of time. In fact, it is unusual for an accused even to know what crime he or she is charged with or, if informed of that, to be permitted a lawyer or to offer a defense.

What is clear, however, is that the vagueness of the kingdom's criminal statutes works to the advantage of the government. Commenting on the *fatwa* that established "corruption on earth" as an offense under Saudi law, an official source explained that it "applied to any individual who breaches the teachings of Islam, undermines security, or attempts to shake the foundations of the existing government." Hundreds have been imprisoned in Saudi Arabia and dozens executed for such "crimes" as criticizing the government, attempting to practice a minority religion, or belonging to banned organizations such as the Committee for the Defence of Legitimate Rights. Amnesty International summed up the situation this way:

> Secrecy and fear permeate every aspect of the state structure
> in Saudi Arabia. There are no political parties, no elections,

no independent legislature, no trade unions, no Bar
Association, no independent judiciary, no independent
human rights organizations . . . there is strict censorship of
media . . . and strict control of access to the Internet, satellite
television, and other forms of communication with the outside
world. Anyone living in Saudi Arabia who criticizes this system is harshly punished. After arrest, political and religious
opponents of the government are detained indefinitely without trial or are imprisoned after grossly unfair trials. Torture is
endemic. Executions, flogging, and amputations are . . . carried out with disregard for the most basic international fair
trial standards.[99]

And this is to say nothing about the treatment of women in Saudi
Arabia, who, in addition to suffering rampant discrimination, can be
repeatedly raped by their employers without avenue for redress or
flogged viciously if accused of "moral crimes."[100]

Saudi Arabia is America's closest Arab ally. One U.S. administration after another has ignored its abysmal human rights practices in
order to preserve the flow of reasonably priced oil and maintain military bases in the Middle East. Nor is it only the government that has
colluded with the kingdom. When Amnesty International tried in
2000 to purchase space in one of Houston's two newspapers for an
ad critical of the Saudi record, both of them, sensitive no doubt to
being in Big Oil's hometown, turned us down.

Myopia is not normally a fatal condition but the events of 9/11
have proven that it can certainly be a threat to a nation's—our
nation's—health. It is not only that fifteen of the nineteen hijackers
were raised in the kingdom or that the corruption of the royal family was a major factor that spurred bin Laden to follow the terrorist
path. It is that the Saudi rulers, terrified that democracy and dissent
might diminish their power and access to wealth, have, like General

Zia in Pakistan, underwritten a strict form of Islam called Wahabbism, designed to keep the population at home under control and burnish the Saudi image with radicals abroad.

Coupled with political repression, this strategy has, at least until recently, discouraged moderate voices and closed off all vehicles for political dissent, leaving violence the only apparent option for those who seek change. "We're not talking about a limited number of people [who support Al Qaeda]," says one Saudi dissident, speaking of the Saudi population. "It's a trend." "If you are the only school of thought," says another, of Wahabbism, "you by nature become increasingly extreme."[101] And also, paradoxically, increasingly vulnerable. Reports of political instability in Saudi Arabia abound, which may be one reason one Saudi prince has called recently for democratic elections in the kingdom and a few dissidents been given a bit longer leash.[102] It may well, however, be too little, too late.

The tragedy is that the hostility toward the United States was far from inevitable. "Arabs are much closer to Americans than Europeans," observed Rami Khouri, a well-known journalist in the region. "Arabs love American culture, the rocket to the moon, technology, fast cars. They love going to America. Now they feel like jilted lovers."[103]

Could the United States have prevented these developments? Not entirely. But our close identification with the royal family, whom their critics consider "Muslim tyrants," has carried with it enormous costs. As Bernard Lewis, an expert on Islam, put it, "Middle Easterners increasingly complain that the United States judges them by different and lower standards than it does Europeans and Americans . . . they assert that western spokesmen repeatedly overlook or even defend actions or support rulers that they would not tolerate in their own countries."[104] How much easier it would be to refute this charge had we taken steps over the past few decades to wean ourselves from over dependence on Saudi oil, thereby freeing ourselves to make advocacy for greater openness in Saudi Arabia a key component of our foreign policy.

• • •

Of course, no matter what posture we struck in the past toward Arab leaders, many in the Arab world would still fulminate against the United States for no other reason than our support of the right of Israel to live peacefully with its neighbors. Arab governments have encouraged, if not sanctioned, anti-Israeli and, by implication, anti-American rhetoric as a surefire way to divert their citizens' attention from the privation and repression they experience every day.

But while the United States' support of Israel's right to exist within secure borders, free of the threat of violence, is entirely admirable, achieving that objective has been undermined by the United States' frequent failure to condemn Israeli human rights violations—a failure that leaves America open to the charge that it promulgates a double standard. Israeli citizens have been subjected to years of wanton bloodshed, and yet Israel manages to sustain a democracy and provides judicial means for the redress of grievances. Such fortitude deserves high praise; suicide bombers unsparing condemnation; and the anti-Semitism that sometimes accompanies criticism of Israeli policies unequivocal rejection.[105] Nonetheless, the fact remains that Israel has been responsible for widespread violations of the rights of Palestinians, as most reasonable supporters of Israel will themselves acknowledge.

"I was always begging the officers to give me another house to destroy," said Moshe Nisim, a member of the Israeli Defense Forces who operated a D-9 Caterpillar bulldozer during the Israeli incursion into the Jenin refugee camp in spring of 2002. "For three days I just erased and erased. . . . The officers warned [the Palestinians] to leave before I entered, but I didn't give anyone a chance to escape. . . . There were many people in the houses when we began to destroy them. . . . I got great pleasure out of every house I took down."[106] Whether it be confiscation of Arab land, the demolition of Palestinian houses even while occupants remain in them, the use of Palestinians as "human shields" or the killing of hundreds of children not engaged in lethal combat, Israel does itself no service, even though it has ample grounds for its own complaints about the deaths of civilians, by engaging in such brutality, a brutality that merely stokes the passions of would-be suicide bombers.[107] Because for every bomber who acts out of religious motives ("This life . . . for God, it's not worth the wing of a mosquito. You cannot compare this life with the afterlife. It's like a drop in the ocean. Why should I waste the ocean for this drop?"),[108] there are others whose reasoning is much simpler. "Why did you want to commit suicide?" Israeli Defense Minister Benjamin Ben-Eliezer asked Arin Ahmed, a would-be suicide bomber who changed her mind at the last minute. "You killed my friend," Ahmed said.[109]

The United States, often quick to condemn Palestinian violence, reinforces suspicions of its own motives and makes the work of serving as an honest broker in the conflict all but impossible when it fails to bring a like measure of outrage to the mistreatment, maiming, and death meted out to innocent Palestinians. That the Israeli-Palestinian conflict is so emblematic for much of the Muslim world, such a test of America's true colors, leads to an inevitable conclusion: although the extremists who seek Israel's destruction will never be satisfied, we should ensure—for pragmatic and moral reasons—that they have no additional grievances with which to sway the moderate or undecided.

• • •

"Washington has much to learn from Algeria on ways to fight terrorism," said William Burns, Assistant Secretary of State for Near Eastern and Northern African Affairs in December 2002.[110] In 1992 the Algerian government declared an election null and void because Islamists were poised to win it. If the Islamists had been allowed to assume power peacefully and forced to cope with the challenges of governing one of the world's poorest and most fractious countries, it is entirely conceivable that, as in Iran today, the extremists might have split into factions, a viable opposition have arisen naturally, and the radicals eventually driven from power. (Islamists are very good at mounting protests but have an abysmal record at actually running countries.) Instead, tens of thousands of people, many of them civilians, were killed by the Algerian government over the next decade in the name of restoring "order." Algerian militants were responsible for manifest atrocities as well, but the government's response to terrorism is hardly one that the United States ought to emulate.

Yet since the events of September 2001 the United States, never a purist when it has come to aligning itself with human rights-abusing regimes, as we have seen, has appeared even less cognizant of the bitter fruit such alliances yield, even less willing than in past years to challenge repressive rulers as long as they were on the right side in the war on terrorism. And one authoritarian government after another, taking their cue from President Bush's declaration of all-out war on all terrorists everywhere, has used that war as an excuse to further erode human rights.

Robert Mugabe's notoriously repressive regime in Zimbabwe, for example, has expelled foreign journalists who have reported critically on his rule. "We would like them [the journalists] to know," a government spokesperson explained, "that we agree with President Bush that anyone who in any way finances, harbours, or defends terrorists is himself a terrorist. We, too, will not make any difference between terrorists and their friends and supporters."[111] Burma (Myanmar), one of the world's most brutal dictatorships, was quick to enroll in the antiterrorist club, declaring it "has been subject to terrorism in the past," no doubt including at the hands of its great democracy advocate, Daw Aung Sung Suu Kyi. China has in effect extracted a *quid pro quo* from the United States, saying shortly after 9/11, "The United States has asked China to provide assistance against terrorism. China, by the same token, has reasons to ask the United States to give its support and understanding in the fight against terrorism and separatism," which is Chinese code language for those who, usually nonviolently, seek independence for Tibet and the Muslim province of Xinjiang.[112] President Megawati Sukarnoputri of Indonesia has used the threat of terrorism as an excuse for that country's abusive crackdown in the provinces of Aceh and Irian Jaya. Under the cover of fighting terrorism, even Australia has taken to refusing entry to political asylum seekers and holding them in deplorable conditions on Christmas Island, 1,400 miles from Darwin.[113]

The United States has continued to speak out against some of these regimes—notably, those less central to the war, like Zimbabwe and Burma—but has far too often given new found allies a "pass." Washington is eager, for instance, to resume military contacts with Indonesia that had been severed due to human rights abuses committed by the Indonesian military in the past and, even more tellingly, has argued in court against a lawsuit that seeks to hold ExxonMobil responsible for rape, torture, and murder committed by that military in conjunction with its protection of Exxon Mobil assets in the province of Aceh. Though the State Department was not required to take a position one way or the other on the lawsuit, it chose to do so because "initiatives in the ongoing war against Al Qaeda" could be "imperiled . . . if Indonesia . . . curtailed cooperation in response to perceived disrespect for its sovereign interests."[114]

Malaysia and its outspokenly anti-Semitic prime minister, Mahathir bin Mohammad, have long been objects of criticism by both private human rights groups and the State Department, but in

May 2002 the U.S. attitude toward this enemy of democracy changed markedly when President Bush received him at the White House and was effusive in his praise of Malaysia's support for antiterrorism efforts. Nor was the president reticent in December 2001 to embrace President Nursultan Nazarbayev of Kazakhstan, despite his government's continuing harassment and torture of its Uighur minority and Nazarbayev himself being suspected by the Justice Department of having extorted millions of dollars from American oil companies.[115] "We . . . reiterate our mutual commitments to advance the rule of law and promote freedom of religion and other universal human rights," the two presidents said in their joint statement, though critics might be excused from the cynical observation that this friendship was founded more upon U.S. desire to secure access to an airbase in Kazakhstan than a sudden discovery that the two both loved human rights.[116] (Not surprisingly, within the following six months some twenty newspapers in Kazakhstan were shut down and opposition leaders beaten.) But perhaps the most dramatic reversal of field had to do with Russia, whose brutality in Chechnya candidate Bush had regularly decried. "Russia cannot learn the lessons of democracy from the textbook of tyranny," he said during the 2000 presidential campaign, and he had vowed no cooperation without "civilized self-restraint from Moscow"—strong language which in his May, 2002 trip to Russia had warped into "We will work to help end fighting and achieve a political settlement in Chechnya," his sole comment on the matter.[117]

It goes without saying that gaining the cooperation of other governments to fight terrorism is a legitimate foreign policy goal. But what the United States seems to forget with great regularity is that by identifying itself with those who abuse human rights—particularly when the rights being abused are those of Uighur Muslims in China, Acehnese Muslims in Indonesia, Uighur Muslims in Kazakhstan, and Muslims in Chechnya—we invite the conclusions that U.S. rhetoric about democracy and freedom is no more than that and that the war on terror is in fact a war on Islam.

And one thing more: we seed a new generation of terrorists. In Uzbekistan, to take one of the most egregious cases, the United States has cultivated a military alliance with a government that is renown for the grotesque nature of its human rights record: people detained without access to lawyers, families, or medical assistance; widespread torture; regular reports of deaths in custody; no dissent; no real elections.[118] "Needless to say," explains one informed observer, "U.S. military aid for antiterrorist activities in countries like Uzbekistan will invariably provide their leaders with resources that can be turned indiscriminately against their own populations. And that, paradoxically, . . . will end up driving the discontented toward the only political alternatives that are radical enough to put up a fight."[119]

Jeffrey Goldfarb, who teaches democracy to foreign students all over the world, reports that, more and more, those students (from South Africa to Ukraine to Indonesia), potentially our strongest allies, are turning against the United States. They see the war on terrorism "being used as a cover by dictators around the world to justify crackdowns on democracy advocates. . . . Suddenly the strategic resources of . . . dictatorships are more important than the lives of human rights activists. Suddenly the defense of the American way of life and our democracy seems predicated upon a lack of concern for the democratic rights of people in less advantaged countries."[120]

It doesn't have to be this way. How much wiser it would be to look to some of our great human rights successes for guidance. In 1987 when the United States was closely identified with an autocratic regime in South Korea, anti-American demonstrations were commonplace among prodemocracy advocates, in spite of the sacrifice American soldiers had made in the Korean War. Gradually that changed. And what made the difference? "The antipathy declined as the United States was no longer seen as supporting repressive military regimes in Korea," said the American ambassador, Thomas C. Hubbard. "Korea is an example of how democratic currents can dissipate heat and anger."[121] Of course no parallel is perfect: Korea was relatively prosperous; it was not threatened by terrorism; and American influence was pervasive. And that support for Korean strongmen still grates: when two fourteen-year-old South Korean girls were run over and killed by an American armored vehicle in 2002, it unleashed an outpouring of resentment attributed at least in part to lingering indignation at the past U.S. alliance with South Korean dictators.[122] But there is still a lesson to be learned here: it *does* matter what company you keep. The United States would fare far better fighting terrorism if it fought more consistently for human rights.

And not just in the civil and political realm. Failed states obviously provide fertile soil for terrorism, but states fail for many reasons. The United States' support for the global fight against AIDS bolsters the struggle against terrorism. Governments whose armies are decimated and budgets drained as a result of the disease can hardly be expected to be paragons of stability or effective stalwarts against violence. Stopping the trade in illegal diamonds in West Africa means stopping the use of proceeds from those sales used to purchase weapons by terrorist cells, including, reportedly, Al Qaeda.[123] And development assistance, if administered wisely and not wasted, can be a powerful tool against terrorism, mired as the retinue often is in poverty and hopelessness. As President Bush's former ambassador to Pakistan put it, "I really believe that creating jobs in this country is a way to protect American lives."[124]

The United States would fare far better if it were a more principled and consistent advocate for human rights. But to be that, we would first need remove the mote in our own eye. We would need to climb out of the cellar when it comes to foreign aid. We are the

nation with the smallest aid budget relative to the size of its economy (about 0.1 percent of GDP) of all the rich nations in the
world.[125] We would need to do away with the death penalty, our insistence upon which is already handicapping the war on terror as one
European ally after another, scandalized by our continued use of a
punishment they regard as barbaric, refuses to extradite or assist in
the prosecution of terrorist suspects who may be subject to execution.[126] Most of all, we would need to employ tactics that respect
human rights in the war against those who would destroy them. But
one of the reasons we are so ambivalent about those who have
cracked down on human rights overseas is that we have so badly
compromised them here at home. It is very difficult to clean
another's face if you are trying to do so with your own dirty hands.

CHAPTER 4

The Haunting of America (II):

How Committing Human Rights
Violations Here at Home Does Us
Damage Overseas

*There shall be one law for the citizen and for the
stranger who dwells among you.*

Exodus 12:49

Anser Mehmood, a citizen of Pakistan, had overstayed his visa
in the United States. There was no question of that. Like thousands
of other immigrants, a majority Hispanic, he had been working ille-
gally here—in Mehmood's case, as a New York City taxi driver and,
later, a truck driver. The United States had every right to arrest and
deport him. Before 9/11, if he had been one of that unlucky minority whom the Immigration and Naturalization Service (INS) had in
fact picked up, he would, most likely, either have been deported or,
if he could show that he had applied for a visa extension, given time
to have his application processed. If he had applied for political asylum here, he would not normally have been forced to leave the
country until that claim had been ruled invalid.

But none of this is what happened to Anser Mehmood because he was one of more than 1,100 Middle Eastern or South Asian immigrants taken into custody by the F.B.I and/or INS in the days and weeks immediately following the attacks of September 11. Arrested on October 3, 2001, Mehmood was transported to the Varick Street Jail in Manhattan. He was told he had overstayed his visa and that he would be taken before an immigration judge the next day. He was also told he could call his wife in a few hours.

But the next day came and Mehmood had not been allowed to contact his wife. Instead, he was visited by the F.B.I., shackled with handcuffs, a belly chain and leg irons, and transferred to the Metropolitan Detention Center (MDC) in Brooklyn. When he arrived in Brooklyn, the authorities attached two more sets of handcuffs to him and another set of leg irons. One of them then hurled him full force against a wall. "Why are you so fat?" a guard asked derisively.

They then forced him to "run" down a long ramp, the handcuffs and leg irons cutting into his wrists and ankles. Placed in a cell, he waited about twenty-five minutes until another guard appeared and threw him against the wall again, this time bloodying his lip. "Do what we say or that will be the end of you," someone snarled. Finally, after his picture was taken, he was again forced to "run" with the restraints still on, then unshackled and given an orange prison suit. "Why have you shaved the hair under your arm?" someone asked him with a sneer. "Do you know why you are here?" someone else inquired. "A visa charge," Mehmood replied, "Naw," came the answer, "You're a World Trade Center suspect."

For the next two weeks Mehmood was held incommunicado. The nature of the charges against him was not clarified. He was finally allowed to call his wife two weeks after his arrest but, when she was not at home to receive his call, he was told that he was only permitted one personal call a month and would have to wait six more weeks to talk to her. (It was three months before she was allowed to visit him.) He was not permitted to speak with a lawyer for seventeen days and in fact made his first appearance before an immigration judge without benefit of counsel.

Held at MDC for six months, much of that time in super maximum security normally reserved for the most dangerous inmates, he occupied a cell whose window had been painted to keep out all natural light. Two cameras were aimed at him twenty-four hours a day. "I was very ashamed and very afraid," he said later. "Every hour here feels like a day, every day feels like a week. And what will happen to my wife and four children? I have lost my American dream—my house, my truck. In all my years as a taxi driver, I never even had a traffic violation."

Finally, Mehmood was charged with using an invalid Social Security card and ordered to leave the country after a secret hearing. He was transferred to Passaic County Jail in New Jersey where in May 2002, eight months after he was taken into custody, he was finally deported to Pakistan. He had never been connected in any way to the events of 9/11. In fact, F.B.I. officials had told him on October 4, 2001, the day after his arrest, that it had no further interest in him, and that was the last time he saw them. Anser Mehmood was no terrorist, not by a long shot. He was an illegal immigrant trying to build a new life for his family. He had broken the law and he deserved to suffer the consequences. But he did not deserve to be mistreated; he should not have been held incommunicado; and his case should not have been kept secret, his circumstances not generally known until Amnesty International finally succeeded in visiting him in April 2002.

Mehmood's case was typical of the post-9/11 immigrant detainees, a class of people, virtually all Muslims, taken into custody shortly after the attacks, sometimes abused, held for a prolonged time without charges being brought against them, often denied prompt access to counsel or contact with their families, their names and hearings withheld from public view. Much of this is in violation of international law and some of it—the abusive treatment, certainly—is in violation of the INS's own regulations. And though 129 of the more than 1,100 immigrants arrested after 9/11 were eventually charged, like Mehmood, with some minor criminal offense, not one of them was ever charged with anything having to do with terrorism.

Under U.S. law, noncitizens cannot claim the same range of rights that American citizens can, but they are not without any. Five days after the terrorist attacks, the rights they *could* claim shrank even further. The attorney general issued a regulation, for example, allowing the INS to hold noncitizens in custody without charge for an unspecified "reasonable period of time" in the event of an "emergency or other extraordinary circumstance," whether they are suspected of terrorist activity or of accumulating a dozen parking tickets.[127] At least 317 of those taken into custody after 9/11 were not charged for more than forty-eight hours; at least thirty-six were not charged for twenty-eight days or more; at least thirteen, forty days; at least nine, fifty days; and in one case for 119 days.[128] Are those "reasonable periods of time," particularly inasmuch as international law provides that "a person shall not be kept in detention without being given an effective opportunity to be heard promptly by a judicial or other authority"?[129] Not knowing exactly what you are charged with and therefore how to defend yourself is bad enough under any circumstances. When it is combined with lack of contact with family, long periods of time without access to an attorney, and the fact that your detention is being kept secret ("Secret arrests are a concept odious to a democratic society," one federal judge ruled[130]), the problems appear insurmountable.

Any government has the responsibility to protect its people from violence. The United States government has argued, for one thing, that deportation hearings must be closed because details that seem innocuous by themselves may be of use to the terrorist network if made public. And maybe that is true. One federal appeals court has agreed. But when a government is targeting one particular ethnic or religious minority for special scrutiny and taking actions that risk violating international human rights standards, it has a particular obligation to step gingerly, to put safeguards in place to mitigate against "mistakes." Due process exists, after all, not to make it harder to convict the guilty but the innocent. And hearings are generally kept open not to garner sympathy but to guard against abuse. Surely it is less likely—not a guarantee but less likely—that authorities will hold someone for 119 days without charge or prevent reasonable contact with families if they know they will have to account for their performance before the courts and the public. If full disclosure risks endangering the citizenry, then let the government make its case to a responsible authority on an individual basis in order to truly separate the wheat from the chaff.

"What we are doing," explained Assistant Attorney General Viet Dinh with reference to the post-9/11 immigrant detentions, "is simply using our process or our discretion to the fullest extent to remove from the street those who we suspect to be engaging in terrorist activity."[131] But not only were no actual terrorists removed from the street by this massive roundup, but hundreds of people who had previously felt no antagonism whatsoever toward this country may have been transformed into adversaries, including nationals from countries like Turkey and Pakistan that had taken risks to support the United States in the war on terrorism and felt betrayed. Mufeed Khan, a Pakistani, had lived in the United States for eleven years, running a small business in Los Angeles. One of 131 Pakistanis deported after 9/11, virtually all for visa violations, Khan said, "For me America was a dreamland. I used to think I was lucky to live in a liberal and democratic country. But the dreamland became hell . . . I was treated badly because I was a Muslim. Carrying a Muslim name should not be a crime."[132] And we may be assured that Mr. Khan did not keep his feelings to himself when he arrived back in Pakistan.

Or consider the case of one of the few non-Muslims taken into custody, Omer Marmari, one of five Israelis who aroused attention because they were taking what appeared to observers to be an excessive number of pictures of Ground Zero and not displaying sufficient reverence for the site.[133] After a week held incommunicado and a total of seventy days in jail, forty-five of them in solitary confinement, Omer was deported to Israel. Over the course of those seventy days, U.S. authorities demonstrated dramatically what is wrong with immigrant sweeps. It seems that at first the FBI did not realize that "Omer" is an Israeli name, different from the Arabic "Omar." They could not tell the difference between speaking Hebrew and speaking Arabic. They did not realize that someone who fasted on Yom Kippur is probably not a Muslim. And even when Israeli authorities finally learned of Marmari's detention and vouched that he had just completed three years of service in the Israeli Army, it still took weeks to win his freedom. "I respected America as the guardian of human rights," said Marmari's mother when he finally returned home. Now she regards it as "a Third World country, like Syria."[134]

The truth is of course that the United States is not anything like Syria (where I would be in grave danger simply for writing a book like this), but when we violate human rights, we make it far harder to convince the world of that. There is nothing inherently wrong with deporting visa violators or requiring foreign nationals to register with their host governments. But if we are going to engage in racial profiling, whether in the detention and deportation of immigrants or the registration of all males over the age of sixteen resident in this country who hail from twenty nations, nineteen of them Islamic, let's remember that such profiling by race and ethnic origin alone is not only a violation of international law but also does immense damage to our relations with the Muslim world, both here and abroad.[135] Pakistan, for example, a key ally in the war on terror, has expressed outrage at the registration and fingerprinting of its nationals in the United States.[136] And such racial and ethnic profiling would not have worked to stop John Walker Lindh, a Caucasian American, Jose Padilla, an Hispanic American, or Richard Reid, a Caucasian British citizen, in any case. At the very least we need to ask ourselves if secret detentions and racial profiling are what America wants to stand for: not promise, but discrimination; not due process, but prejudice; not liberty, but chains. Surely there is a better way.

In June 2003, the Justice Department's office of inspector general agreed. After reviewing the treatment of more than 750 aliens taken into custody after 9/11, the watchdog agency concluded that there were "significant problems" in how the detainees had been treated.[137] Fidel Castro, for one, found no such "problems," however. When he cracked down on peaceful dissidents in Cuba in March 2003, he did so with a simple rationale. He was pursuing the same policies the U.S. had after 9/11, Cuban officials said—rounding up dangerous elements.[138]

• • •

For more than fifty years, one of the most highly respected means to chart a "better way" in human relations, at least during the course of war, has been the Geneva Conventions, which regulate the conduct of war and treatment of war prisoners. The four conventions (1949) along with two protocols (1977) make up what is known as the "humanitarian law of war." One hundred eight-five countries, including the United States, are parties to the four conventions, which constitute one of the most widely agreed-upon set of international norms. For any party to breach the conventions is considered a mark of singular dishonor.

Beginning in the fall of 2001, hundreds of prisoners taken into custody during combat in the Afghanistan War were transported by the United States to our military base in Guantanamo Bay, Cuba. By the fall of 2002, the number stood at 583 from some thirty-three countries, including six prisoners captured in Bosnia. According to the Defense Department, these prisoners included both Taliban and Al Qaeda fighters, "the worst of the worst," in Defense Secretary Rumsfeld's words, "among the most dangerous, best trained, vicious killers on the face of the earth," so dangerous that they had to be hooded and strapped in one position for the twenty-hour flight from Afghanistan to Cuba and then housed in small individual cells at the base. At first blush one might assume that, since they were taken in the course of combat, the detainees at Guantanamo were prisoners of war and hence subject to the Third Geneva Convention Relative to the Treatment of Prisoners of War. If that were the case, the prisoners, while they could be interrogated, would only be obligated to give name, rank, birth date, and serial number (as any aficionado of old war movies knows); would have to be "quartered under conditions as favorable as those for the forces of the Detaining Power who are billeted in the same area"; could not be prosecuted merely for participating in hostilities (though they could be prosecuted for war crimes or crimes against humanity); and would need to be released at the "cessation of hostilities," that is, at the end of the war.

But these conditions did not make the Bush administration happy. For one thing, the United States wanted to interrogate the prisoners for information about terrorist networks and potential future attacks. Under the conventions, prisoners of war are to be held in quarters roughly equivalent to those of the occupying powers, but to provide such relative comfort might well be a disincentive to cooperation. For another, the United States wanted to preserve the option of trying them for participating in terrorist acts (which could certainly be considered crimes against humanity) but, if they are prisoners of war, they are subject to court martial, just as American soldiers would be for such crimes, not special military tribunals. And for a third, since war had never been formally declared by the United States Congress and since, that fine point aside, the president had announced that the United States would not stop fighting until terrorism had been destroyed, and since therefore it was not clear that "cessation of hostilities" would ever come, even though the war in Afghanistan was effectively over, and since in any case the United States did not want to let anyone go who might be a future threat to the country, the provision of the convention requiring repatriation of prisoners at the close of war was not one the United States was eager to implement.

The solution therefore seemed simple: declare that, though they might have been taken prisoner in the course of a war, these prisoners were *not* prisoners of war. They were what the administration called "unlawful combatants" to whom the conventions did not apply.

That conclusion may well have been correct. A strong argument can be made, especially in relationship to the Al Qaeda prisoners, that they do not fit the definition of "armed forces" that the conventions require. They were of course not fighting under the flag of a state that had ratified the conventions. They were not subject to a system of command that enforced compliance with international law. They did not distinguish themselves from civilians by wearing a uniform or other distinctive sign and they did not carry arms openly. On the other hand, the Taliban soldiers *did* meet many of these criteria and Afghanistan *was* a state party to the conventions. The status of the prisoners, then, was murky. But on one point, the third convention is clear. If there is doubt as to who is or is not a prisoner of war, the decision is not to be made by the captors. The decision is to be referred on a case-by-case basis to a "competent tribunal," like an international or civilian court. But that was something the Bush administration refused to do.

It is still a mystery why. For it is very likely that, had the question been referred to a court, and certainly an American one, the Defense Department's wishes, at least in regard to the Al Qaeda prisoners, would have prevailed. But whether because the administration could not be certain of the outcome or because it did not want to reveal certain information to a court or because it holds international law in disrepute, the referral was never made. And so the United States, long a defender of the conventions, now stands in breach of them. It has also denied the Guantanamo prisoners access to attorneys and has argued in federal court, thus far successfully, that because the Guantanamo camp lies outside U.S. territory, federal courts have no jurisdiction and the courts therefore no power to intercede.[139] The prisoners find themselves in legal limbo.

But why should we care? Many of the prisoners at Guantanamo no doubt *are* "vicious killers"; we may all be far safer with them behind bars. Yet the decisions to ignore the Geneva Conventions and deny the prisoners due process carry with them at least three serious implications. First, they mean that more than 600 people, including, we have subsequently learned, children as young as thirteen, are being held indefinitely without an opportunity to prove themselves innocent or harmless. Some of them, we now know, were indeed both. In March 2002, Lt. Col. Bill Cline, deputy camp commander at Guantanamo, admitted that some of the prisoners were "victims of circumstance" and probably innocent.[140] A week later Maj. Gen. Michael Dunlavey, the top officer in charge of anti-terror intelligence, described some of the prisoners as "lost souls" who could provide no worthwhile intelligence.[141] At least seventeen have attempted suicide. In October 2002, three Afghani prisoners were released. Two of them were over seventy years old, one so addled that he babbled as a child and claimed to be 105.[142] In March 2003, eighteen more were let go; in May 2003, more than twenty more. If these were "the worst of the worst," the United States had little to worry about. Except perhaps how many other innocent people were being incarcerated with no foreseeable end in sight. Given that more than 100 people convicted in U.S. courts of capital crimes and sentenced to death have subsequently had their convictions overturned, it is not hard to imagine that, if one of the world's best judicial systems can err as frequently as ours does, the odds are enormous that "convictions" *without trial or hearing of any kind* are likely to result in manifold injustice. It does the United States no good to be associated with that in the eyes of the world and especially in the minds of the Muslim public.

Nor, secondly, to be seen to be violating international law when it serves our purpose. The State Department has regularly criticized regimes in places like Egypt and Pakistan for holding prisoners—many of whom these governments would label "terrorists"—in indefinite detention in violation of international due process standards. Our behavior at Guantanamo provides such governments a veil of sanction for their own miscreant deeds and sends a signal that, regardless of what we profess, we believe that international agreements like the Geneva Conventions apply to us only when it is convenient.

And that signal, thirdly, may have dire consequences for U.S. service men and women who, in the course of what President Bush has repeatedly described as a long war against terrorism, may fall into the hands of our adversaries. In those circumstances, the conventions, while far from a guarantee that captive members of the U.S. military will not be mistreated, may be the best shot we have. They seem, for example, to have helped protect American POWs held by the Iraqis in the recent war there. But if Americans are ourselves seen to have shredded those international covenants, we are in a far from enviable position when we wish to invoke them on our own citizens' behalf.

What is happening at Guantanamo, then, is a powerful illustration of why human rights (in this case, the right to have your status as a prisoner determined by a "competent tribunal" or the right to counsel) do not depend upon their claimants being virtuous human beings. Fundamental human rights adhere to you even if you are the worst creature on earth. In the long run, every one of us is better off that way, whether we are inside the prison camp looking out or outside trying to protect ourselves and our children from the capricious use of power. For if the United States engages in such use, it makes it that much easier for the terrorists to do likewise—in their recruitment schemes, for one, and their ideological screeds, for another.

• • •

With its relish for indefinite detentions, the United States government would like us to think that to be an "unlawful combatant" is to be without any rights whatsoever. But the Supreme Court decision of 1942 (*Ex parte Quirin*) upon which the administration bases its use of the term "unlawful combatant," did not authorize open-ended confinement; it only established that "unlawful combatants" were subject to "trial and punishment by military tribunals" rather than civilian courts. Moreover, while *Ex parte Quirin* was decided years before the Universal Declaration of Human Rights (1948) and other international protocols that codify due process for those accused of crimes were created, Article 75 of the First Additional Protocol to the Geneva Conventions (1977), says that "persons who are in the power of a Party to the conflict and who do not benefit from more favorable treatment under the conventions," that is, have not been declared prisoners of war, still have rights to such things as trial "by an impartial and regularly constituted court"; the right to mount a defense, to be presumed innocent, to not be compelled to testify against themselves and to examine witnesses.[143]

Perhaps in recognition that there may come a day when the United States wishes to try one or more of the Guantanamo prisoners or some others taken into custody in the course of the war,

President Bush in November, 2001 established military tribunals or commissions to hear cases against alleged terrorists.[144] It becomes difficult at a certain point, after all, to continue contending that prisoners are indeed dangerous criminals who ought never be released if you have never proved your allegations in a court of law.

As with indefinite detention, the United States has regularly condemned countries that utilized military tribunals, rather than civilian courts, to try those accused of terrorist crimes, such as Peru in its first trial of American citizen Lori Berenson or Nigeria in its prosecution of environmental activist Ken Saro-Wiwa. Nonetheless, the U.S. tribunals were authorized by executive order and their rules of procedure issued by the Defense Department in March 2002 (Military Commission Order No. 1).

Order Number 1 provides for practices that conform to many of the rights recognized in the First Additional Protocol, but the tribunal system also contains several troubling flaws. The president or the secretary of defense will alone decide who will sit on the commissions and who will be tried before them. The defense secretary or the presiding officer may close the trial proceedings to press and public in order to protect classified information, intelligence sources, or the physical safety of those involved and the defendant and his private lawyer, if he has one—if not, he will be provided a military lawyer—may be excluded from such closed portions of the trial. And the verdicts, including sentences of death, may not be appealed to a civilian court but only to a review panel appointed by the secretary of defense with a final decision by the president (who instigated the case in the first place). This means that an individual can be executed—itself a gross violation of human rights—after a trial from crucial portions of which he was excluded and without appeal to any independent authority.[145]

Furthermore, military tribunals would be reserved for non-U.S. citizens, while Americans charged with terror-related crimes would be tried in civilian courts with the full range of protections those courts allow. *Except* of course (and here is the inconsistency) when non-U.S. citizens like Zacarias Moussaoui, the so-called "20th hijacker," are tried in civilian courts, and American citizens, like Jose Padilla, who is alleged to have plotted to explode a radioactive "dirty bomb," and Yaser Hamdi, originally a Guantanamo prisoner, are labeled "unlawful combatants," held in military brigs and told that they are not entitled either to legal counsel or a trial, military or otherwise. They are simply entitled to sit in a prison cell until they die or the United States decides to do something else with them.[146]

What is going on here? It is all very confusing. But then it is meant to be. Because the moment someone is put on trial before *any* kind of court, the government has implicitly recognized a claim to rights (the right to counsel, for example), limited though they may be. What the United States is trying to do in the war on terrorism is to deny as many rights to alleged terrorists as it can possibly get away with. And the way it is doing that is by treating its adversaries sometimes as warriors and sometimes as criminals, whichever suits the government better, thus creating a hybrid model—one day, a criminal justice model; the next day, a war model—for the prosecution of the "terrorism war."

Under a war model, prisoners taken in combat are considered prisoners of war and entitled, as we have seen, to treatment appropriate to POWs. They can be held in detention without trial until "cessation of hostilities" but cannot be prosecuted for noncriminal acts committed in the course of war (such as responding to U.S. military attacks on Afghanistan). The United States does not want to accord prisoners taken captive in the war on terrorism such status, however (it does not want to have to release them at the "cessation of hostilities," for one thing), so it resists labeling them POWs and calls them "unlawful combatants" instead.

Unlike POWs, "unlawful combatants" *can* be prosecuted for hostile acts committed in the course of war, but then they are entitled to a trial—at least a military trial, as required by the criminal justice model. But the U.S. is not comfortable bringing most of them to trial either, whether because it fears providing information to its adversaries or doesn't think it can win its cases, so it adopts with respect to "unlawful combatants," that portion of POW status that allows for detention without trial. The Defense Department may inadvertently have revealed how committed the administration is to keeping the criminal justice and war models jumbled up with one another when William J. Haynes II, the Pentagon's top lawyer, proclaimed that even if a defendant brought before a military tribunal were acquitted, he "may not necessarily automatically be released." "When somebody's trying to kill you or your people," he went on, "and you capture them, you can hold them."[147]

We have created, then, with respect to these prisoners a vicious circle, a perfect Catch-22. And in the process the administration has come close to successfully undermining some of the most basic human rights commitments with which the United States has long been associated: imprisoning two American citizens while denying them the rights to know what they are charged with, to seek legal counsel, and to be subject to *habeas corpus*. At a time when the United States is representing itself as the defender of freedom and respect for the rule of law, you need not be concerned that something like that will ever happen to you or your loved ones in order to see what is wrong with it.

• • •

Keeping the line between warriors and criminals murky serves what the United States perceives to be its interests in the world at large, not just in prisons. Nothing illustrates this better than the fatal attack on six men carried out in Yemen on November 3, 2001 by a C.I.A.-controlled Predator drone aircraft. The principal target was Qaed Salim Sinan al-Harethi, whom the United States believed to be Al Qaeda's chief operative in Yemen and whose name was on a list of alleged terrorist leaders President Bush has authorized the C.I.A. to kill on sight wherever they are found. When the missile hit al-Harethi's car as it drove through the desert, five other men, including an American citizen, Ahmed Hijazi, were killed as well.

These six men may all have been very dangerous and their deaths no cause for mourning. If they could be considered enemy soldiers and it could therefore be said that they were killed in the course of military action, there would be little reason, from a human rights perspective, to question the C.I.A.'s action. But if they ought to be considered criminal suspects, then the authorities have an obligation at least to try to take them into custody so that they can be charged with a crime and put on trial. If in the course of attempting to take them into custody, the lives of the authorities or innocent people in the vicinity are in danger, then, as a last resort, lethal force is permissible, and if the suspects are killed, so be it. But if criminal suspects are killed without any attempt to apprehend them and therefore without their having an opportunity to defend themselves in a court of law, their deaths might be considered assassinations or what is technically called "extra-judicial executions." No wonder President Bush has declared his a *war* on terrorism even though Congress has declared no such war, and no wonder the United States is so eager to pin the label *warrior* on its terrorist adversaries.

But if every suspected terrorist anywhere in the world is a warrior and not a criminal and hence subject to elimination by executive fiat, then the whole world is a battlefield and innocent people almost inevitably will lose their lives along with the guilty. If every suspected terrorist is a warrior, then why bother to take anyone into custody, including for example, U.S. residents, like the so-called "Buffalo Six"? Why not just kill *them* on sight?

If the United States can unilaterally authorize the liquidation of a target without need for formal safeguards or legal process, then so can any other country in the world. Israel has already done it, to the past consternation of the United States, and many more would surely be tempted to follow suit. Such vigilantism would make for even more chaos than we face today, with no place in the world immune from somebody's designation as a legitimate military theater and no leaders, including our own, exempt from nomination as legitimate targets. What provoked such sympathy around the world about the attack on the World Trade Center was that it was quite evidently a civilian rather than a combat target and was filled with innocent people. In the adoption of this "kill on sight" strategy, we are sacrificing our standing to maintain such important distinctions.

This is not to say for a moment that terrorism does not require a rethinking of human rights concepts. Terrorists do not identify themselves with just one country or one battlefield. They do not operate in the open. They are very different from traditional warriors, and it may therefore be necessary to adopt new rules for dealing with them. The debate about when to treat this struggle as a criminal one and when as a military is complicated. But such a debate must take place—in the Congress, at the U.N., in the public realm—before one nation decides unilaterally to rewrite the old rulebook. For if the United States, without any consultation, appears to be flaunting international law and acting without moral or political restraint, we hand our adversaries *prima facie* evidence that our commitment to pursue the fight against terrorism in the name of defending the rule of law is mere rhetoric. And if that happens, the struggle to defend a civilized world will ultimately be lost, no matter how many "enemy combatants" we kill in the process.

• • •

No human rights crime is more common than torture. It is practiced in something like two-thirds of the countries of the world. The United States is one of them. Male prison guards have been guilty of systematic rape of female prisoners, for example; some police departments have been notorious for their brutal treatment of suspects. But until the war on terrorism, no one could seriously assert that such practices were either commonplace or *de facto* policy—at least not at the federal level. Until, that is, the United States began taking Al Qaeda operatives into custody and holding them on air bases and in detention centers overseas that are beyond the reach of U.S. law.

Now credible reports have emerged, denied by top officials but widely confirmed by agents in the field, that some detainees are kept kneeling for hours, held in awkward, painful positions or are "softened up" by being beaten, blindfolded, thrown into walls, and subjected to constant loud noise. When U.S. officials are not themselves administering such degrading treatment, we are apparently transferring the prisoners—"rendering," it is called, like stripping flesh from a bone—to allied intelligence services in Egypt, Jordan, Morocco, and perhaps elsewhere, that have long histories and much practice in utilizing torture during interrogation[148]

All this is rationalized in the name of procuring information to protect innocent people from being maimed or killed by terrorists who, after all, have been proclaimed the epitome of evil, demonic even, and hence unworthy of their captors' restraint. We will examine this issue in far more detail in chapter 7. For now it is sufficient to ask just one question: what will tarnish America's reputation as a defender of all that is humane more quickly than to gain a reputation as a practitioner of this beastly crime?

Torture eats away at the torturer as well as the victim. Whatever small gains might be made in intelligence (and, as we shall see, they are small indeed, if they exist at all) are more than offset by a loss of self-respect and an erosion of the norms that would guide a civilized society. Political conservatives, who often champion the importance of such cultural norms, ought to be the first to see that. Torture is no way to build a better world and it is no way to keep us safe.

• • •

Since September 11, 2001, many new practices have been introduced in the name of greater security. Some of these, such as tighter screening at airports and better coordination among intelligence-gathering agencies, make perfect sense, despite the occasional dust-up. A staff member of Amnesty International USA, for instance, was questioned at some length shortly after she had boarded an airplane because she was seen reading a set of newspaper clippings collected under the title "Human Rights in the News" and some fellow passenger had apparently found such reading suspicious.

But other new measures are more worrisome. Here are some examples:

- The USA Patriot Act, passed shortly after 9/11, permits the FBI to ascertain what books an individual checks out of a library or purchases in a bookstore. Already close to 10 percent of all public libraries, in one survey, reported having been approached by federal or local law enforcement seeking such information.[149] The Patriot Act also authorizes F.B.I. agents to infiltrate worship services or political gatherings even if there is no demonstrable reason to suspect any criminal activity. It expands the F.B.I.'s power to conduct phone and Internet surveillance even as the Bush administration proposes that Internet providers be required to build a centralized system to monitor the use of cyberspace.[150]

- More than two dozen people, including several American citizens, have been detained for months without charge, held as "material witnesses" in terrorism cases but not charged with a crime and hence unable to defend themselves, seek bail, or argue for exoneration.[151]

- Organizations, including charities, that the government suspects of helping terrorists can be closed down based on classified information ("secret evidence") that the organizations and their attorneys are not allowed to see and hence have no capacity to refute.[152]

- Prison officials can now monitor communications between detainees and their lawyers without obtaining a court order if the attorney general finds that there is "reasonable suspicion" a prisoner may communicate with a lawyer "to further or facilitate acts of terrorism."[153]

- The government apparently maintains a "no fly" list of individuals whom airlines are advised not to allow onto planes. It is not clear how one's name gets on such a list (or how to get it off!) but thus far the list has snagged, among others, the chairwoman of the Green Party of Maine and a 74-year old Roman Catholic nun named Virginie Lawinger who has long been a political activist but is far from a terrorist.[154]

Perhaps we can at least take comfort that Attorney General Ashcroft's attempt to suspend the writ of *habeas corpus* altogether—something he proposed in the aftermath of the attacks—was not approved by Congress.

• • •

A little more than a year after he became a hero on September 11, 2001, Shahram Hashemi, whose story I told at the outset of the previous chapter, was required by the INS to report to its office to be photographed and fingerprinted. It is not that Hashemi had done anything wrong. Unlike Anser Mehmood, his visa was perfectly in order. But Hashemi is an Iranian, one of thousands of men from those twenty selected countries, nineteen of them predominantly Muslim, whom the United States now wants to register and fingerprint *en masse.*

Hashemi, who had been in the United States for four years already, was chagrined. Humiliated. He couldn't sleep. "I am not afraid of fingerprint [sic]," he said. "But the foreign students being educated here, like me, are the best potential allies for the United States when we go back to our native countries. We have seen this great democratic system. But this act [the registration] just typecasts these students in a way that's degrading."[155]

Ultimately, Hashemi decided to cooperate. But this hero of 9/11 did not feel good about the matter and neither should we. As another Iranian, who had been in this country since 1997 and had had an application for permanent residency pending for five years, said after he had gone to register and been held in jail overnight before his father-in-law freed him on bond, "This was the most embarrassing thing that ever happened to me. I am very respected in the business community, and I was just trying to do the right thing. . . . We were treated like animals in Iran, and all I want is for my kids to grow up and say they're proud to be Americans. But until the day I die, I'm going to be a foreigner in this country because of the way I look and my accent."[156] It is enough to make the Statue of Liberty shed tears.

In its "anything goes" mentality in the fight against terrorism; its inclination to downplay, if not ignore, even the most egregious human rights violations of its allies; its tendency to see terrorists under every turban; its conviction that international covenants mean little and matter less, the Bush administration has done more to damage human rights in its two and a half years in office than the occasional hypocrisy and frequent indifference of nine previous presidents put together. And it has done so largely with the acquiescence of the American people.

Part of that passivity is attributable to fear, to the assumption that the violation of other people's rights is necessary in order to keep Americans safe. But part of it is also due to confusion about what human rights are, where they come from, and where respect for them will lead us. It is to those basic questions about the nature and implications of human rights that we now turn.

PART II GROUNDWORK

CHAPTER 5

What Makes Rights "Right"?

The Origin of Human Rights
and the Challenge of Universality

I follow a thread till I find something I was looking for. When I find it, I stop.[157]

V.S. Naipaul

One of the factions in the early Christian Church, followers of the charismatic preacher Montanus, believed that only those who ate a steady diet of radishes would be saved. The women in the community, who played an inordinately powerful role in the life of the movement, especially promoted this healthy regimen. Had Montanism prevailed, Christians might eat vegetables at Holy Communion rather than wafers, and the Roman Catholic church might suffer today no shortage of priests. But, whether it was resentment of roots or of "rabble," the church fathers of the day overruled the ordinances of the Montanist women and declared Montanists enemies of the church in AD 170 and that was, for all intents and purposes, the end of that.

Why did the Montanists fade into history? Did God really have no taste for radishes? Was it somehow a violation of natural law for

women to assume a leadership role in the Church? Or did the
Montanists simply lack the power to build an adequate consensus
for their views? Had they been operating in China where a saying
has it that "only those who appreciate root vegetables can know the
true meaning of life," might the story have been different?

Whether it be a religion, a nation, or the world at large, the norms
that govern at any one point in history reflect the views of those who
are at the moment holding the prevailing mantle of power. It can be
a small and elite group of people or a much larger conglomeration,
so large in fact that the elite are discouraged from challenging them.
The latter is the case with regard to human rights, as we have seen
earlier. But in either instance the question arises as to how we
decide what rights are "right." Upon what authority are human
rights based? There are really only three possibilities: God, natural
law, or philosophical pragmatism, which is sometimes referred to as
political consensualism or constructivism. This question about the
basis for human rights is not just an esoteric philosophical one.
Whichever we pick will have profound practical implications, not
least of all for U.S. foreign and human rights policies.

From the standpoint of those of us active in the human rights
movement, it would be wonderful if the source of human rights was
behind door number one: "God." If we could prove to the satisfaction of the world that some universally recognized deity had imbued
human beings with a set of rights that happened to coincide with the
thirty articles of the Universal Declaration of Human Rights
(UDHR), such that even the most enthusiastic atheist would pros-
trate herself before that tablet, my job as executive director of
Amnesty International USA would suddenly become a lot easier.
But, alas, given the enormous diversity of the world's faiths—when
they are in need of spiritual guidance, the Asmat people of
Indonesian New Guinea, for example, pay homage to their deceased
family members by using their skulls as pillows, a practice one can

safely assume would be frowned upon by other religions which prefer to allow their dead to rot in the ground or burn on the funeral
pyre[158]—it is a reasonable bet we will not reach consensus upon a
religious basis for human rights any time soon. If individual people
of faith wish to believe that God is the source of human rights, they
are welcome to do so, but, absent demonstrable proof, their faith is
unlikely to be sufficient to convince everyone else.

Which leads us to the second possibility, natural law. Sometimes
natural law and the theological conviction that God determines
human rights shade into one another, theologians claiming that God
works his will through human nature, but, for simplicity's sake, we
will treat the two arguments separately. Might it be, then, as advocates of the natural law approach would argue, that all human beings
share certain traits—reason has been a popular candidate—that distinguish us from other entities, both sentient and inert, and hence
make us eligible to claim certain rights? This clearly was the view of
America's Founding Fathers who famously made reference in the
Declaration of Independence to "the laws of Nature" as the source
of the rights to "life, liberty and the pursuit of happiness."

The objections to natural law as a basis for rights are long-
standing. It is not difficult, of course, to demonstrate that all
human beings share certain characteristics. But finding those that
constitute the "essence" of being human and are of sufficient
import to serve as a rationale for rights is a bit harder. "What is
man," asked Isak Dinesen, "but an elaborate machine for turning
red wine into urine?" As far as we know, that capacity is indeed
shared by every human being, but the sardonic suggestion that it
is what is most important about the human creature is one that
most sober people are likely to reject outright.

But who says that "sober people" get to decide this question? In
fact, how do we choose who gets to determine which human characteristics are "essential" enough to ground a set of rights and which

rights they ground? The Founding Fathers may have thought that Nature's law implied rights to life, liberty, and the pursuit of happiness, but what do we say to a social Darwinist who believes that Nature's law implies nothing more than territoriality, aggression, and the survival of the fittest?

The history of natural law theory would suggest that conceptions of human nature have varied wildly throughout the ages, that they will continue to vary far into the future, and that the ones that have predominated at any one time have done so far more for political than philosophical or scientific reasons. In the Middle Ages, for instance, the law of Nature was interpreted by the Roman Catholic church to condemn usury. Most church property at the time was in the form of land, and landowners, because their wealth is not liquid, need to borrow money. So "naturally" they opposed usury and conveniently found Natural reasons to do so. But with the rise of Protestantism, drawn primarily as it was from the middle class (i. e., the "lending class"), Nature suddenly had a change of heart and was understood to look with favor on usury. Or to take another example: the great champion of natural law, John Locke, reflecting the prejudices of his time, famously believed that the rights derived from Nature only inhered in the propertied classes and that hence women and peasants could make no claim to them. And what do we do with the ancient Uro people of Peru who did not believe they were human at all and hence would *a priori* reject any notion of human nature? We tell them they are wrong because the majority of us say they are wrong. The first problem with a natural law theory of rights is that what is "natural" (and hence "right") ends up being so largely in the eye of the beholder. Little wonder that natural law was long the favored justification of the elite classes for the denial of rights to the oppressed.

Even if we were to hit upon a common human characteristic of note that everyone agreed upon, however, we are next confronted with a second problem, the philosopher David Hume's classic contention that we cannot derive an *ought* from an *is* (the so-called "naturalistic fallacy"). Grant for a moment that "reason" is what makes humans distinct (ignoring growing evidence that the higher mammals use reason, too, and the simple observation that newborn babes and brain-damaged adults may not), how does that "fact" alone lead us to any conclusions about how human beings should treat one another? In order to claim that creatures who reason should *ipso facto* be treated with dignity, for example, we need to insert the unverifiable moral claim—unverifiable at least in any logical, mathematical, or scientific sense—that the Good consists of treating creatures who reason with dignity.

It is easy to see why the insertion of a moral judgment between a statement of fact (an indicative) and a statement of what we would like to see happen (an imperative) is so crucial. Consider that some anthropologists regard kin selection, the tendency to maximize our genetic line by favoring our genetic relatives in proportion to the genes they share with us, a "natural" human trait. Without some moral intervention, that "natural" trait could lead to a simple right to protect one's immediate family from harm, but it could just as easily lead to a right to revenge myself on the murderer of my child by impregnating that murderer's daughter, thereby perpetuating my genes.[159]

Which brings us to a third problem with natural law, assuming we have successfully navigated our way through the shoals of the naturalistic fallacy, namely, how do we get from a very general statement about human nature (human beings are characterized by reason) to a detailed list of rights specific enough to guide us in our day-to-day lives? How does the general trait of utilizing reason help us decide whether people have a right to a fair trial or to claim a nationality or to marry without limitation due to race or gender? Couldn't a reasoning creature decide that it would be best to recognize not a right to a nationality but only a right to claim world citizenship? For these and other reasons, natural law has long been out of favor as a basis for human rights.

Yet despite all these objections, some neoconservatives want to resurrect it. Francis Fukuyama (of "End of History" fame) is one of the most articulate exponents of this view. According to Fukuyama, "Any serious discussion of human rights must ultimately be based on some common understanding of human ends or purposes." And yet Fukuyama's account of natural law displays every one of the three weaknesses described above.

When it comes to the failure of theories of human nature to imply a concrete set of rights, for instance, Fukuyama acknowledges that "There is no *simple* translation of human nature into human rights" and "Human nature does not dictate a single, precise list of rights." As for the naturalistic fallacy, which Fukuyama wants to discredit, his account proves its cogency. "While violence . . . may be natural to human beings . . . ," Fukuyama says at one point, "so is the propensity to control and channel violence." Leaving aside the question of how Fukuyama knows that "the propensity to control and channel violence" is a natural phenomenon and not behavior learned over many generations, we may wonder how he gets from the human capacity to control and channel violence to the conclusion that this is a good thing. "Human beings reasoning about their situation can come to understand the need to create rules and institutions that constrain violence in favor of other natural ends," he explains. But what is that reasoning and what are those rules if not moral judgments about human rights inserted between the *is* of violence and the *ought* of constraint?[160]

And what exactly is this human nature that underlies human rights? One looks in vain through Fukuyama's writings for a precise description of it. This is as close as he comes: "What gives us dignity and a moral status higher than that of other living creatures . . . cannot be reduced to the possession of moral choice, or reason, or language, or sociability, or sentience, or emotions, or consciousness, or any other quality that has been put forth as a ground for human dignity. It is all these qualities coming together in a human whole. . . . "[161]

Yet if Fukuyama's definition of human nature is fuzzy, the political conclusions he draws from it are anything but. For, like John Locke assigning privilege to the propertied, Fukuyama's notion of human nature leads to precisely the type of society he himself wants: "Human rights that speak to the most deeply felt and universal drives, ambitions, and behaviors will be a more solid foundation for political order than those that do not," he says. *"This explains why there are a lot of capitalist liberal democracies around the world at the beginning of the twenty-first century but very few socialist dictatorships* [emphasis added]" Here Fukuyama has revealed his hand. Not because there is necessarily anything wrong with the triumph of liberal capitalist societies (that is a different question) but because human nature, vague as his conception of it is ("moral choice, reason, language, sociability, emotions, consciousness," etc.), has been used to justify his political preconceptions. History had "ended," after all, in Fukuyama's famous conception, with the victory of capitalism over socialism.

People of widely disparate political views advocate natural law theory but neoconservatives particularly love it because it is imprecise enough to allow them to pick and choose the rights they like and discard the ones they find inconvenient. How interesting that, though the biological needs for food and shelter are probably the common human traits least difficult to establish, neither Fukuyama nor his neoconservative counterparts would ever be caught dead arguing that social and economic rights (as opposed to the right to property and corporate competition) are indisputable imperatives derived from human nature. Nor is it likely that neoconservatives will ever conclude that the death penalty is a violation of Nature's laws or that gay, lesbian, bisexual, and transgender people have the "natural" right to full expression of their sexuality.

But if natural law is not the philosophical basis for human rights, that leaves political consensus. It is precisely because everyone gets to participate (at least through the medium of his or her governments) in the making of human rights under this option that some partisans of natural law disdain it. The academics, the elite, and the economic and political mandarins of power determine what natural law sanctions. What the political consensus approach conceives of as human rights emerges from a cacophony of many voices, power spread wide—from the makers of human rights treaties to the judges of human rights laws to the human rights activists struggling for justice on the ground.

And what is it those voices are trying to agree on? Is it "human ends or purposes"? No. Why should we need to come to consensus on those controversial topics in order to agree that torture is wrong? You and I can both be against torture even if I believe that the purpose of life is to get into Heaven and you believe it is to avoid being bored. Despite our differences, we can both very well agree that we would rather not live in a world in which torture is commonplace. That is because human rights are not dependent upon our sharing the same notion of God, the same religion, philosophy, or conception of human nature; they are dependent upon our sharing a commitment to what makes for a civilized world.

We are all familiar with cartoons of a caveman holding a woman by her hair and dragging her along the ground behind him. Let's assume for argument's sake that at some point in history behavior like that was commonplace (and not just the product of a cartoonist's imagination) and that no one alive at the time, male or female, questioned it. During such an era, women had nothing like a "right" not to be treated in that fashion. In fact, we can hardly be critical of the cavemen because, if no one expressed any doubts, they cannot be blamed for doing something no one at the time thought of as wrong.

But gradually the practice of dragging women around by their hair dissipated. It was hardly because some philosopher came along and convinced the cavemen that, because women were creatures who could reason, they should be treated with respect. It was no doubt for far more practical reasons than that. Perhaps the cavemen realized that women were little good to them all bruised and battered, less fit to perform women's tasks, less likely to bear healthy progeny. Or perhaps women found some clever ways to stop the mistreatment. Nobody knows of course, but, whenever and however that happened, at that point the understanding of what constituted acceptable behavior—what today we would call "civilized" behavior—took a great leap forward. In some way, these new norms worked better.

Over the centuries, largely in response to political tyranny and repression, growing numbers of people have found their voices and their power and, as they have, norms of reputable behavior have evolved. At the time of the Aztecs, human sacrifice was acceptable. It no longer is. In the Middle Ages pouring boiling oil over your enemies was understood to be standard operating procedure in warfare. It no longer is. Slavery was commonplace for thousands of years. Gradually it, too, was outlawed. Some of these developments are attributable no doubt to changing moral or religious beliefs and others to quite pragmatic reasons, such as a recognition that societies are unstable without some rules to govern them, or that if you pour boiling oil over me, next time I may well do the same to you. Economic realities have no doubt also played a major role: if you grow food I need to survive and I am not strong enough to take it from you, it may well serve us both to agree on some ways to trade fairly. Whatever the reasons for their development, norms have changed and our understanding of civilized behavior, of what a just society looks like, has changed with them.

Today those norms of civilized behavior, that description of a just society, are codified in the form of human rights. In a funny kind of way human rights constitute a universal set of manners, a worldwide book of etiquette, that the structures of power ought to abide by in their treatment of the people over whom they rule. Human rights are designed to protect the less powerful from the whims and caprices of the mighty. They provide protections that have been judged to work to make societies more equitable, peaceful, stable. The fact that the power elites often fail to heed their manners, that abhorrent practices like slavery are still found in the world, does not mean that they are judged tolerable by the world community as a whole any more than the fact that murders still occur means that laws against murder are meaningless.

In one important respect, human rights are very different from traditional etiquette, however. When I was in theological school, a particularly fusty old professor taught us that, when you paid a pastoral call at the home of a parishioner and the parishioner was out, you left your calling card on the butler's tray with the card's right top corner folded down if you intended to call again later that day and its left top if you would wait for the morrow. Since I only served a few years in the parish ministry, never had a parishioner wealthy enough to employ a butler, and would never in any case have paid a pastoral call without phoning first, I never got to put this arcana into practice. But I always wondered who decided which corner meant what. (Readers, be warned: I may have gotten the corners backward so, if you find yourself faced with a butler, just leave your message verbally!) The truth is that, when it comes to etiquette, we rely upon a very small group of Emily Posts to interpret a very narrow set of axioms.

But when it comes to human rights, we look to the collective experience of humankind, as interpreted by what is called, to the jeers of its critics, the "international community." By this we do not mean of course all humans on earth. We can't poll everybody to determine the rules for a just society and, if we did, some rights we recognize today might not receive a majority. By "political consensus" we do not mean unanimity. But we do mean a growing circle of people—women, the dispossessed, minority cultures—whose voices are becoming louder and who are claiming a greater share of the power. And we do mean those international and regional institutions, preeminently the United Nations but also such bodies as the European Parliament, that give those voices a hearing and help articulate human rights principles. And we do mean all those international covenants and conventions such as the Geneva Conventions, the International Covenants on Civil and Political Rights and on Economic, Social and Cultural Rights, the Convention Against Torture and Other Cruel, Inhuman or Degrading Treatment or Punishment, the African Charter on Human and Peoples' Rights, and dozens of others, as ratified by the nations of the world, that codify those principles in law. We do mean those international and regional courts, beginning with the Nuremberg court but including today the European Court of Human Rights, the Inter-American Court of Human Rights, and several others that interpret those international human rights laws. And we do mean those international nongovernmental organizations like Amnesty International and Human Rights Watch that help monitor violations of those laws and encourage the enforcement of them.

Is this truly a "community"? Some do not think so. The freelance critic David Rieff has asked, "What thinking person can take seriously the idea that there is such a thing as the international community? Where are the shared values uniting the United States and China, Denmark and Indonesia, Japan and Angola . . . ? Of course there is an international order . . . and there are international institutions . . . but the reality is that the international community is a myth. . . ."[162]

To determine whether Rieff is right, it will be helpful to consider in what ways it makes sense to call any place—say, Bismarck, North Dakota—a community. It is certainly not because every single citizen agrees with the predominant values that govern Bismarck's life. There are no doubt porn shops in Bismarck that most citizens would decry but that manage to stay in business nonetheless. It is not because of the citizenry's geographical propinquity to one another, because we all know people who have lived away from their hometowns for thirty years but still consider themselves part of that hometown community. No, a community is a community because in some more or less formal way it self-identifies as a community and adopts, again more or less formally, a set of common goals, directions, traditions, norms, and values, that at least the leadership and large numbers of the citizenry of the community profess to share. In this sense Bismarck did not become a true community overnight but gradually grew into one.

In exactly the same way, the international community has, over the past fifty or sixty years, begun to self-identify as a community. This doesn't mean that every country, much less every citizen, shares the same goals, directions, traditions, norms, or values, but it does mean that gradually a shared sense of identity and values is emerging that much of the world's leadership and many of its inhabitants profess to share. Which of those values do the United States and China have in common? At least in their legal statutes, an aversion to torture and, more and more, a recognition of the right to private property. Denmark and Indonesia? Among others, an unwillingness to execute the mentally retarded. Japan and Angola? Along with all but two other countries in the world, ratification of the Convention on the Rights of the Child. The construct of an "international community" and the values that flow out of it are still evolving, far from complete. In some ways, the notion of an international community may be no more than a term of convenience, but terms of convenience can still point to real phenomena and, while Mount Olympus is a myth, Narnia is a myth, and Atlantis is a myth, Bismarck is not and neither is the international community.

Rieff's skepticism is that of a professional critic but others have less admirable motives to doubt the existence of an "international community." Condoleeza Rice, as we have seen, has called it "illusory." Those who wish to see the United States dominate the globe are naturally resistant to recognizing an extra-American authority, a broader court, whether it be of opinion, policy, or justice, before which the United States might actually be called to account. Far more convenient to understand the grounds of human rights as embedded in natural law—a law that Americans can define as they see fit; that, arguably, provides our favored political system, liberal capitalist democracy, with the imprimatur not just of history's blessing but of human nature itself, and that implies only the vaguest of prescriptions for what rights will be recognized. It makes sense, too, that those who wish to premise human rights on the worthiness of those who would claim them will tilt toward natural law. Because if human nature is the basis for human rights, then those whose humanity we can question—those who are part of the "world of evil," in the president's words, or, more graphically, "barbarians," in the vice president's—have forfeited their rights by forfeiting their humanity. It is no coincidence, then, that natural law (or a combination of religious and natural law arguments) constitutes the authority for human rights that those who favor a Messianic role for the United States in world affairs most prefer.

This does not mean, of course, that the approach to human rights I have called political consensus is without its own challenges. Rights derived from such consensus, are not fixed and determined for all time. But then neither are notions of God or Nature's law. Human rights at the international level rely upon much the same principle the Supreme Court invoked when it determined that "evolving community standards," concerning what constitutes pornography or whether it is acceptable to execute the mentally retarded, influence the interpretation of justice. This means that theoretically, at least, the arc of the universe may *not* always bend toward justice, may *not* become progressively more enlightened, and human rights standards might conceivably regress. The best we can say is that past experience seems to show that the more people who are involved in the standard setting (that is, the more widely the power to set standards is shared), the less likely the backsliding. Some day, I suppose, a social consensus might reemerge that it was acceptable for males to drag females around by their hair. But the more power, political, economic, and cultural, that women accumulate, the less likely the possibility.

Naturally it would be splendid if we could determine what rights are "right" based on a commonly accepted standard of truth rather than having to rely upon a process that is dependent upon the wider and wider distribution of power. Unfortunately, deciding what is "true" has rarely been as simple as Georges Clemenceau made it out to be when he replied to a question as to what historians would say was the cause of World War I: "I do not know what they will say was the cause of the war, but I do know that they will not say that France invaded Germany." (Had Clemenceau never heard of revisionism?) Rights that are grounded in international consensus—even "semi-sensus"—and elaborated in formal treaties and conventions are far more likely to be perceived as politically legitimate than notions of what God or Nature do or do not justify.

The greatest challenge to political consensus as the basis for human rights, however, comes from those who charge that our current conceptions of human rights are not in fact universal but reflect a distinctive Western bias. If the human rights community cannot respond to the critics who champion various forms of cultural relativity, the whole human rights enterprise is in serious jeopardy.

• • •

Perhaps no practice has more dramatically focused the debate over the vaunted universality of human rights than that of female genital circumcision (FGC), the removal of parts or all of the clitoris and/or portions of the labia, an operation found widely throughout Africa as well as in parts of Asia and some immigrant communities in the West. Even the name for the ritual is controversial, those who condemn it insisting that it be dubbed "female genital mutilation." Strict cultural relativists have argued that FGC should be tolerated out of respect for the cultural traditions it reflects. The American Anthropological Association articulated the principle underlying this view in 1947 as the UDHR was being contemplated. "Standards and values are relative to the culture from which they derive," the association warned, "so that any attempt to formulate postulates that grow out of . . . one culture must . . . detract from the applicability of any Declaration of Human Rights to mankind as a whole."[163]

The strict view of cultural relativism is fairly simple to refute. It rests upon the assumption that tolerance of alternative customs is a positive value. But that assumption is itself culturally based. Millions of fundamentalist Christians, Hindus, Muslims, and Marxists, who believe that their views ought to be imposed on others, would be scandalized by the presupposition of the cultural relativists that diversity is good in and of itself. If the cultural relativist is to be intellectually consistent, she must admit that the "standards and values [of cultural relativism] are [themselves] relative to the culture from which they derive."

Of far greater import to the human rights enterprise than this flawed intellectual criticism is the notion that conceptions of universal human rights, derived as they are largely from the Western Enlightenment tradition, are at odds with understandings of human rights inherent in other religious and cultural traditions and hence have no applicability to people living under the influence of those other traditions. Saudi Arabia abstained on the vote on the Universal Declaration of Human Rights in 1948, to take but one example, largely because it found the declaration's views of women and the family and on the right of the individual to change his or her religious beliefs to be at odds with its perspectives. Some Asian leaders have argued vociferously that Asian culture puts greater emphasis upon the needs of the community than the rights of the individual and that hence the civil and political rights of individuals should be subsumed to the social and economic development of the larger society. Radical Islamists contend that *shari'a* law ought to govern social and political relations in Muslim societies and that governments should be held accountable for its enforcement, even when its strictures (about the severity of punishments or the role of women, for instance) are at odds with universal human rights.

Schooled as we in the West are to respect cultural diversity (the value, as we have just seen, upon which the strict relativist position is based), these arguments carry a certain appeal but, in the face of the threat of terrorism, they engender profound confusion as well. If we try to impose our views on others, won't that merely create resentment and encourage a dangerous backlash against us? Isn't that kind of "cultural imperialism" exactly what I have been criticizing in earlier chapters? Yet, at the same time, if more democracy and human rights is, as I have argued, an important element in the struggle for the hearts and minds of the terrorist retinue, how can we ignore their violation? Isn't that *also* what I have condemned?

This dilemma underscores the importance of the argument for human rights from a political consensus or constructivist point of view. There is no question of course that many of the rights understood today to be universal are products of the Enlightenment and consistent with the Western liberal tradition. But it is important to remember in the first place that the articulation of those rights in the form of the UDHR was by no means a Western undertaking alone. The eight-nation drafting committee included among its most prominent members Dr. Peng-chun Chang of China. The Human Rights Commission that was charged with producing the declaration was composed of Egypt, India, Iran, and Lebanon, among others. The declaration itself incorporated a whole series of social and economic rights such as the right to food, housing, medical care, and employment not traditionally associated with the Western conception of rights and which still remain controversial in some Western contexts.

Moreover, the U.N. that adopted the declaration consisted of thirty-seven member nations that stood in the Judeo-Christian tradition, eleven in the Islamic, six in the Marxist and four in the Buddhist. Only eight nations abstained on the vote. Six of those were the Marxist nations, which objected to the recognition of any individual rights that could be asserted over against the State; one was South Africa, which was wary of the declaration's being used to invalidate its apartheid policies (as, indeed, eventually it was); and only one was Muslim—Saudi Arabia. Despite the cultural diversity of the assembled states, not a single one voted against the UDHR.[164]

Since 1948, growing numbers of states, from every religious and cultural tradition, have ratified additional human rights treaties, covenants, and conventions.[165] Just as important, human rights principles as articulated in the UDHR and its offspring have been incorporated into dozens of national constitutions. As a result, in many cases human rights abuses don't just violate universal standards; they violate the laws of the very countries in which those abuses are found. Torturing dissidents in China, for example, violates that country's constitution, no matter how loudly Chinese leaders proclaim that individual rights are subordinate to social. When it comes to torture in China, we don't even need to appeal to "universal standards" to find grounds for condemnation; we can just ask the

Chinese to obey their own laws. Female genital circumcision is against the law in at least half of the countries in which it is found; the laws just often go unenforced.

But is it even the case, as those who question the universality of human rights principles would have it, that those principles are in fact at odds with non-Western religious and cultural traditions? In some cases a *prima facie* case can be made that they are. For those in the Muslim tradition, for example, who interpret *shari'a* law to require the stoning to death of Amina Lawal, the young Nigerian woman who bore a child out of wedlock and risks being killed for her act of adultery while at the same time the father of the child suffers no consequences, the universal human rights principles that require equal protection before the law and ban cruel, inhuman, and degrading punishment are without force or meaning.

But most religious and cultural traditions encompass a wide variety of opinions as to what those traditions require. The Muslim human rights scholar, Abdullah Ahmed An-na'im, has insisted, for example, that *shari'a* law represents an "historically conditioned interpretation of Islamic scriptures" and that new understandings are necessary in light of contemporary developments. The general principle of *qawama*, the guardianship and authority of men over women, he says, is based upon "two conditions: men's [physical] advantage over and financial support of women." The first of these "is not relevant in modern times where the rule of law prevails over physical might" and the second is rapidly changing.[166] Similarly, the renowned economist and philosopher, Amartya Sen, who was born in India, has sharply disputed the contention that "Asian values" preclude respect for individual civil and political rights. In support of his claim he has cited, among other things, Confucius' observation that "the way to serve a prince" is to "tell him the truth even if it offends him" and the commitment of the Indian emperor Ashoka in the third century B.C. to tolerance of diverse religious sects, limitations on slaughter in war, and "non-injury, restraint, impartiality, and mild behavior" toward all creatures as the mark of good government.[167]

Even if the prevailing views in a particular tradition tend to contradict universal human rights standards, however, that need not mean that those standards are inapplicable. For human rights, as we have argued, are designed to give voice to the voiceless, to set boundaries beyond which the structures of power may not go in their treatment of the less powerful. If this is the case, then the question we must always ask when confronted by a religious or cultural practice that contradicts universal human rights is, "How many people had a say in the shaping of it?" And specifically, "Did the victims of the oppressive act approve it?"

Those non-Westerners who object to the Western bias of universal human rights are almost always the non-Westerners wielding the greatest power in their societies and rarely the non-Westerners on the receiving end of it. Never have I heard a Chinese political prisoner argue that because Asian values champion the right to development over the right to be free of torture, Chinese prison guards are welcome to switch on the electroshock weapons. But isn't that prisoner just as Asian as that guard? Daw Aung San Suu Kyi, who has fought for years for democracy in Burma (Myanmar) ardently disputes the notion that Asian cultural values somehow invalidate the promise of democracy and human rights that she and her movement have been relentlessly pursuing. "Unless they wish to call the people of Burma 'un-Asian,'" she says, "they cannot call our struggle 'un-Asian.'"[168]

The truth is that one of the most promising developments in the human rights movement over the last fifteen or twenty years is an explosion in the number of indigenous human rights groups, even in the most repressive countries, and these groups are helping redefine and modernize exactly what their traditions stand for[169]. When the American legal scholar Ronald Dworkin visited China in 2002 and asked a group of Chinese teachers and students if they disagreed with

the presuppositions upon which human rights rest in Western democracies: namely, equality between persons and autonomy of the individual, virtually all of them insisted that there was no important difference
between Western conceptions of human rights and their own.[170]

Not everyone would agree, of course. Sometimes those who have
experienced what others would consider human rights abuses, such as
female genital circumcision, defend the presumably abusive practice.
Older women in many African communities, who have themselves
been circumcised, usually are the ones who perform FGC and think
it perfectly acceptable. But it is also true that during the American
Civil War, Southern slaveholders often cited the fact that some slaves
defended slavery as a reason to maintain the institution. William
Lloyd Garrison challenged that quaint theory by saying, in effect,
"Give them their freedom and see if they ever try to give it back."[171] In
similar vein, one wonders whether those women who claim to find
nothing problematic in FGC would hold the same view if they had not
undergone the operation (which almost always occurs when they are
children) and could live their lives with their genitals intact. While it
is always dangerous to make cross-cultural, to say nothing of cross-
gender, assumptions, it is worth pondering whether those women who
have experienced FGC and still espouse it would stick to that view if
women who had not undergone the operation were regarded by powerful males in the community as equally desirable or eligible for marriage as those who had.[172] In any case, the key point is that everyone
ought to participate in the setting of human rights norms free from
coercion and with full honor paid to their autonomy. This is especially
true of those whose life experience the norms are designed to address.

What do we who support the universality of human rights say,
then, to those who charge that those rights reflect Western bias? We
say that human rights are guides to civilized conduct that have been
drawn up and recognized by people from all over the world; that
they are incorporated into the laws and policies of vast numbers of

the world's nations; and that they are codified by international law and interpreted by international courts. We say that, while great respect must be paid to individual traditions, human rights ultimately trump all parochial interests, for they are a means by which all people "everywhere in the world," the weak as well as the strong, may give legitimacy to their needs and aspirations.

Fukuyama and other proponents of natural law contend that an approach grounded in political consensus has no grounds for condemning "abhorrent practices like suttee or slavery or female circumcision" because it provides "no transcendent standards for determining right and wrong beyond what any particular culture declares to be a right."[173] But, on the contrary, consensualism reflects not what a "particular culture" regards as right but what the international community has declared to be just. In the face of suttee (a Hindu widow cremating herself on her husband's funeral pyre), slavery, and female circumcision, we have a far better answer than the highly contestable notions that "God dislikes them" or "They contradict natural law." We have an answer that is demonstrable to everybody: "Your practice violates the closest thing we have to agreement among the world's people as to what constitutes cruelty and, because of that, the international community rebukes you."

The way to avoid cultural imperialism is to ground our human rights values not in sectarian notions of the Divine and not in ephemeral definitions of human nature but in the evolving standards of a worldwide civilization. Those standards include social and economic rights (reflecting the interests of the community), as well as civil and political (reflecting the interests of the individual). They are not for the United States or any other country to enforce alone; their realization is the responsibility of everyone. Just as it makes no sense for a white, upper-middle-class American like me to be lecturing indigenous women on the need to reject FGC when instead I should be supporting those indigenous people who are themselves questioning the ritual, so it makes no sense for the United States to throw its weight around in the name of defending human rights without offering all the support it can to those international mechanisms designed expressly for that cause.

Some will inevitably resent criticisms of their customs and practices, no matter who it comes from. No one should be naive about the extent to which recognition of the rights of women, much less of sexual minorities, will cause friction in many parts of the world. Nor should we pretend that respect for social and economic rights will come easily in the United States. But the more that others see this country promoting human rights in a global context, as values shared worldwide and not just derived from the Judeo-Christian, American, or even Enlightenment traditions, the less danger there will be of a backlash against the United States for "telling others how to live their lives."

Such a multilateral approach is possible no matter what one's theory of the basis for human rights, but a consensualist theory demands it. If you believe that human rights are grounded in political consensus rather than God's judgment or Nature's law, it is untenable not to recognize as well that the imperatives derived from rights apply equally to everyone. That is why how we think about human rights philosophically has profound implications for U.S. human rights policy, for if we adopt a consensualist view, we must, if we are to be consistent, subject ourselves to the same standards to which we hold others and allow others to hold us to them as well. By reinforcing the true universality of human rights, such an approach undercuts resistance to rights by terrorists or anybody else and ultimately makes us all safer. But it also requires us to rethink our understanding of a very touchy question—the question of whether there are limits to the reaches of sovereignty.

ar was what happened after it was over. For all intents and pur-
oses the Thirty Years' War struck the death knell of the Holy
oman Empire, which, before the war, had stretched from France
o Poland. Far more important, however, the agreement that finally
ut an end to the bloodshed, the so-called Peace of Westphalia,
stablished once and for all a principle with which the world has
een struggling ever since: the principle of national sovereignty. No
onger would the states of Europe have to defer to a "universal
aonarchy" in making decisions about laws, taxes, war, and peace.
ow they would each be free and independent of the other.

From one point of view, this sounds quite ducky. After all, the
Ioly Roman Emperors were hardly known for their progressive pol-
ics. But there were more than three hundred states in Germany
lone at the time of the Peace Westphalia, most of them ruled by
ieir own autocratic prince or ecclesiastic. Not only could those
tates never agree on common policies but there was no longer any
entral authority to enforce the laws across the region, no matter
ow unenlightened those laws might be. For many of the citizens of
lurope, the Peace of Westphalia resulted in the exchange of one
iighty tyranny for hundreds of petty ones, each pursuing what they
egarded as their narrow individual interests. The result for
lermany was another century of chaos.

Though the concept of national sovereignty has been refined
ver the years, many of the fundamental issues that emerged from
ie Peace of Westphalia have remained. Prominent among them has
een the tension between respecting a state's right to make deci-
ions regarding its own citizens and interests and recognizing that
ome common ground rules that apply to all may be necessary for
ie flourishing, if not survival, of civilization.

That tension is built into the very fabric of the U.N. Article 2,
aragraph 7 of the U.N. Charter declares that "Nothing contained
1 the present Charter shall authorize the U.N. to intervene in

CHAPTER 6

When Wickedness Is in Fa

National Sovereignty and
International Justice

We run a uniquely benign imperium.[174]

Charles Krau

The Thirty Years' War (1618–1648) was one of the m
plicated conflicts in history. I remember spending several hug
trating nights in high school trying to sort out the fates of the H
Holy Roman Emperor, Matthias (who was tossed out a wi
Prague), from the Calvinist Elector Palatinate, Frederick V (
the battle of the White Mountain). I am sure I am a lesser pe
never having gotten it all straight, but I take comfort in the fact
eminent historians, throwing up their hands in despair o
attempt to explain the war's causes and chart its participants, co
it to "the croquet game in *Alice in Wonderland* where the pla
the necks of flamingoes for mallets and hedgehogs for balls."

If I never got quite clear in high school about who kille
and why, I did understand that what was most important al

matters which are essentially within the domestic jurisdiction of any state. . . . " Indeed, it is likely that, had that provision not been inserted into the charter, the organization would not have come into existence in the first place. The U.N. was founded in reaction to two horrific wars *between* sovereign nations, and it envisioned its role as preventing more of such carnage. But it did not take long before the world body was confronted with the fact that much of the worst conflict took place *within* nation states, the Korean War being the earliest and most dramatic example.

When it came to wars, however, even civil wars, the problem of intervention was not so complicated. Wars were understood almost by definition to fall outside solely "the domestic jurisdiction of any state" and Article 1, paragraph 1 of the U.N. Charter had made it clear that the purpose of the United Nations was "to take effective collective measures for the . . . suppression of acts of aggression and other breaches of the peace."

Human rights violations, on the other hand, were another thing entirely. Even long after the adoption of the Universal Declaration of Human Rights (UDHR), how a government treated its own citizens was regarded as "essentially within the domestic jurisdiction" of the state. Despite the growing body of international human rights law, countries, under the guise of national sovereignty, could harass, persecute, torture, starve, and even kill large segments of their own populations and fear little greater rebuke than a resolution of condemnation from the U.N. Human Rights Commission. And, given the inconsistency of the commission and the tendency of the great powers to protect their allies, even the odds of that were pretty slim. As had been the case ever since the Peace of Westphalia, claims of sovereignty were used to cover a multitude of sins.

Over the last ten or fifteen years, however, the balance between national sovereignty and the assertion of international authority has begun to shift once again. With the conclusion of the cold war, East and West had less incentive to offer cover to petty autocrats. The fall of apartheid South Africa in the early 1990s, at least in part as a result of widespread international opprobrium, provided a case study for how multilateral action might end human rights abuses. More democracies in the world brought louder calls for more accountability, in the form, for example, of the South African Truth and Reconciliation Commission. Growing recognition of the global nature of both environmental threats and economic opportunities meant a growing recognition of the interdependence of the planet. Guilt over the genocide in Rwanda in 1994—a genocide that took place while the United Nations slept, the United States having supplied the Sominex—prompted a reexamination of when military intervention was justified. That same guilt may well have prompted NATO's intervention in Kosovo. The decision of the Law Lords in the United Kingdom in 1999 that Augusto Pinochet could be held accountable by Spain for crimes committed in Chile spurred the movement to invoke the doctrine of "universal jurisdiction," as sanctioned, for example, by the Convention Against Torture, the principle that any country may prosecute those who are accused of torture and certain other human rights crimes. Belgium cited that doctrine in 2001 when it convicted four Rwandan citizens of crimes committed in the 1994 genocide. And the International War Crimes Tribunals for the former Yugoslavia and for Rwanda went about their business trying those accused of atrocities in those tragic places.

But swing toward international accountability as the pendulum may, the sovereignty of nations still has plenty of defenders. Two of the most resolute are China and the United States. In 1991 a white paper from the Information Office of the State Council in Beijing put the Chinese position straightforwardly: "China has firmly opposed . . . any country interfering in the internal affairs of other countries on the pretext of human rights . . . China has always maintained that human rights are essentially matters within the domestic jurisdiction of a country."[176] And while the United States has never been quite so explicit in its official statements, it has regularly attached reservations to its ratification of international human rights treaties asserting in effect that the Constitution, as interpreted by the Supreme Court, trumps all international obligations under those treaties. This means that, whether it be "cruel, inhuman, or degrading treatment," as defined by the International Covenant on Civil and Political Rights (ICCPR), or the recruitment into the military of those under the age of eighteen, as precluded by the Optional Protocol on Armed Conflict of the Convention on the Rights of the Child, the United States has generally claimed that where international strictures butt up against national prerogatives, the national invariably prevail.[177]

But what is good for the American goose is surely not good for other countries' ganders when it comes to the war on terrorism. The Bush Doctrine—that there is no distinction between terrorists and regimes that harbor terrorists and that both are equally subject to sanctions—gives no truck to sovereignty as a defense. Because terrorists have to be based somewhere and often operate in collaboration with governments, those who would stop terrorism will almost inevitably violate other nations' sovereignty in the process—in military pursuit of adversaries, obviously, but also, as the Bush administration has demonstrated, in preemptive strikes against would-be purveyors of weapons of mass destruction, assassination of suspects, gathering of intelligence, or imprisoning of foreign nationals without trial. One of the great paradoxes of the war on terrorism is that at the very time the United States is most determined to defend its own sovereignty from attack, it is more inclined than ever to violate the sovereignty of other independent states. President Bush made this explicitly clear in his 2003 State of the Union address with regard to states "that seek and possess nuclear, chemical, and biological weapons," remarks that were aimed at Iraq but could include a host of other countries that "seek or possess" such weapons as well.

And yet the sovereignty-accountability debate is not an easy one for human rights advocates, either. For though we may well share the opinion that sovereignty ought to offer no protection to those who commit serious human rights crimes, we also know that when that intervention takes military form, it can result in enormous havoc and suffering.[178] We know that unregulated intervention would mean endless conflict. We know that to do away with the protections of sovereignty altogether is to invite the most powerful countries to dictate to the weaker. And yet we are also aware that failure to stop mayhem can lead to greater instability and ultimately a government's collapse, and that terrorism may very well sprout where weak governments are spawned.

It is important, then, to get a handle on this question of the relationship of sovereignty to human rights. At the nub of the debate is the question of under what circumstances military intervention is called for to stop human rights abuses. As we shall see, the best answer requires strong affirmation of the authority of the international community—something that, as we have outlined previously, has suffered grievous blows since the events of September 2001.

• • •

What happened in the small Central African country of Rwanda in the spring of 1994 continues to haunt me. I had been executive director of Amnesty International USA for about a year when the genocide began. For one hundred days, machete-wielding Hutus killed some 800,000 Tutsis and moderate Hutus in the worst genocide since World War II. The story has been told eloquently by Samantha Power in her Pulitzer Prize-winning book, *"A Problem from Hell:" America and the Age of Genocide*. Power spares no one. Not the *genocidiares* of course who committed the atrocities. Not the politicians and military leaders in Rwanda who encouraged them. Not the radio station that broadcast the names, addresses, and license plate numbers of those who were to be tracked down and killed. Not the United Nations peacekeeping office (then headed by the current Secretary General Kofi Annan), which insisted that the U.N. soldiers on the ground avoid combat at any cost. Not the Belgian government, which provided 440 of those soldiers and withdrew them after ten of them were killed. Not the U.N. Security Council, which refused to authorize intervention. And especially not the United States, which, fearing another Somalia, insisted on that international passivity; pettifogged endlessly over use of the term "genocide" to describe the massacres for fear its use would trigger treaty obligations compelling intervention; and finally even refused to jam the lethal radio broadcasts because to do so would cost $8,500 an hour.[179]

But Power pulls no punches about the failure of human rights organizations either and here is where my own guilt kicks in. The reason the United States government was so silent was because the Congress, the press, and the American people were so silent. And the reason the latter three made no noise was because the human rights community, and especially Amnesty International, which claims 300,000 members in the United States, was unsuccessful in impressing upon our leaders the magnitude of the horror.[180] We spoke and wrote and petitioned, but we should have been leafleting neighborhoods, pounding on desks, and marching. There is one criterion that has long been recognized as essential to justify military intervention to stop human rights crimes. As a 1905 textbook on international law put it, the cruelties in question must be sufficient to "shock the conscience of mankind."[181] In order to register such shock, human beings often require a push. All of us who neglected to push hard enough in 1994 share in the blame.

If you doubt for a moment that the Rwandan genocide falls into the category of crimes that legitimize outside intervention, just reflect on the following confession from a man named François held at Central Prison in Kigali, the capital of Rwanda, for his part in the atrocities, and imagine similar situations being repeated tens of thousands of times:

> A car drove by with a loudspeaker saying that all Hutus had to defend themselves, that there was a single enemy: the Tutsis. I heard that. I jumped out of bed, grabbed a club, I went out, and I began killing. There was an old woman nearby, with two young children who had not reached school age yet. We took them outside and made them stand by a pit. . . . I killed the children and [a man named Sibomana] killed the old woman. Then we climbed back out [of the pit] and found an old man hiding behind the house. I knocked him out with a club . . . I did not know the people I killed very well. All we were told was to hunt down the Tutsis, and we began to slaughter them. . . . While I was killing, I thought there was no problem, no consequences, since the authorities said the Tutsis were enemies. My neighbors were Tutsis, we used to share everything like water. There weren't any conflicts between us. I don't know why all those things happened. Wickedness was in fashion.[182]

At a minimum, then, when wickedness is in fashion sufficient to shock the conscience of humanity, military intervention may well be justified.

But clearly this is not enough, if for no other reason than, as we have just described in the case of Rwanda, the conscience of humankind is notoriously unreliable. Rwanda may be the most obvious case in recent history in which intervention would have been justified to stop human rights abuses, but it is hardly the only place that has witnessed shocking wickedness. What other criteria for intervention might there be?

Over the past few years, this question has received wide-ranging attention from such disparate bodies as the Stanley Foundation, the Council on Foreign Relations and an International Commission on Intervention and State Sovereignty funded by the Canadian government in response to U.N. Secretary General Annan's challenge to the international community to reach consensus on when and how the world should respond to massive human rights violations. The relative degree of unanimity among these observers is remarkable for such a controversial topic. Here are three widely shared conclusions.

Sovereignty Entails Responsibility. No matter the predilections of some visionary activists and starry-eyed philosophers, the sovereign state as the principal organizing structure for the world's inhabitants is here to stay—at least for the foreseeable future. Nor is that entirely a bad thing. In many ways, sovereignty protects liberty, and anyone who has dealt with the New York State Department of Motor Vehicles is hardly likely to favor a bureaucracy that takes in the whole globe.

On the other hand, if we are to prevent the most serious human rights abuses from taking place, we need to place some limits on sovereignty to protect the common interests of the international community. Parenthood provides a telling analogy. Virtually all cultures recognize that parents have a great deal of latitude when it comes to rearing their children. Article 16 of the Universal Declaration of Human Rights affirms that "Men and women of full age . . . have the right to marry and to found a family" and goes on to say that "the family is the natural and fundamental unit of society and is entitled to protection by society and the State."

Yet no matter how respectful we may be of parental prerogatives, virtually all societies also recognize some limits to parental authority. If a child is being abused or neglected, if a child is being deprived of an education, or if a parent fails to attend to a child's health such that the child's life may be in danger or the child may become a purveyor of disease—in all such instances state authorities have a widely recognized right to intervene, even to the extent of taking custody away from the parents. Parental claims are not unconditional ones; they entail a measure of responsibility as well.

Similarly, with the recognition of national sovereignty by the international community, principally through membership in the U.N., come certain expectations. These may be characterized in different ways. Kofi Annan has said that the U.N. Charter is designed "to protect individual human beings, not to protect those who abuse them."[183] Annan knows that the charter restricts intervention in matters "essentially in the domestic jurisdiction of the state" but he argues that sovereignty vests also in individuals. By implication, to the extent that a state violates the latter type of sovereignty, it sacrifices some of its claims to the former. The Commission on Intervention and State Sovereignty puts it slightly differently: "In signing the [UN] Charter, [a state] accepts the responsibilities of membership. . . . There is no transfer or dilution of state sovereignty. But there is a necessary re-characterization: from *sovereignty as control* to *sovereignty as responsibility* [for the welfare of its citizens]."[184]

Whichever formulation we prefer, the bottom line is this: massive human rights violations, if left unchecked, often destabilize a country or a region; they can result in enormous environmental, economic, and health consequences for the world.[185] But even when their impact is limited to those immediately affected, they send a profound message to others who may be contemplating comparable evil—you, too, can get away with murder. And the more murderous thugs we have at loose in the world unworried about impunity, the more likely it is that they will commit war crimes and crimes against humanity. The more likely it is, in other words, that eventually the U.N.'s obligation to preserve the peace will be put in jeopardy. In light of all this, stopping the most serious human rights crimes is almost always not only a matter of a shocked conscience but of pursuing the common interests of humanity.

If an individual sovereign state is unable or unwilling to exercise its responsibility to protect the sovereignty of its citizens, then it is up to the international community to do so for it.

Military Intervention Is a Last Resort. Nations have been interfering with each other's sovereignty for years—diplomatically, economically, politically. Virtually all observers agree, however, that *military* intervention must always be a last resort, undertaken only when all lesser measures have failed. This is in part because of the danger that with military action the cure will be worse than the disease. Moreover, most countries will commit their troops to battle only under the most dire of circumstances.

A wise question to ask ourselves of any military intervention is "Is it likely to be successful and to make the situation better?" In Rwanda, General Romeo Dallaire, the Canadian commander of U.N. troops on the ground, believed, quite reasonably, that he could stop the slaughter with just a few thousand more soldiers. The genocide was, after all, being implemented almost exclusively with clubs and knives. But the U.N. Security Council denied even that modest request.[186] Thousands have been killed in Chechnya, on the other hand, but no responsible observer has ever suggested outside military intervention there. A nuclear-armed Russia would hardly take kindly to such interference, and the result could be far more catastrophic than the tragedy that has already been unfolding.

The violations that qualify for potential intervention, then, must be only of the most solemn variety, and there must be good reason to think that they will lend themselves to military resolution. Former Deputy Under Secretary of Defense Dov Zakheim has argued against virtually all interventions because "most democracies were not built in a day" and American-style democracy "cannot be forced down the throats of those unwilling to emulate us, no matter how long our forces patrol the streets of their cities and towns."[187] But Zakheim is setting fire to a straw man. Human rights leaders would never advocate using military force solely to impose democracy. Grievous as the denial of the right to vote might be, for instance, or even repression of the press or of political dissidents, those abuses by themselves are insufficient to trigger military action. The Commission on Intervention and State Sovereignty has identified two circumstances that justify intervention: (1) "large scale loss of life, actual or apprehended, with genocidal intent or not, which is the product either of deliberate state action, or state neglect or inability to act . . . ; or (2) large scale 'ethnic cleansing,' actual or apprehended, whether carried out by killing, forced expulsion, acts of terror or rape."[188] Whether or not that formulation is definitive, it signals the gravity that must attend such intervention. The final, critical question is, "Who gets to decide how grave is grave?"

Intervention Must Be Sanctioned by the International Community. We would live in a close-to-perfect world, I suppose, if every nation, no matter how powerful, had to worry that it would be subjected to sanctions of one kind or another if it violated its citizens' human rights. The hard reality is that, to the extent military intervention is on the table at all, it is the stronger countries that are in a position to enforce human rights standards against the weaker. If there is to be any order and consistency to how that happens, if in the name of human rights the world is not to sink into even more chaos than it already has, such action ought to carry the approval of some international authority beyond the nation or nations doing the actual intervening. The intervention ought, in other words, not be unilateral but be taken in the name of the international community just as, theoretically, the United States is to go to war only with congressional authorization, not just presidential, violated though that constitutional provision so frequently has been.

The ideal body to authorize such action is the U.N. Security Council. When it gives its imprimatur, flawed though the council be by the inequity and clumsiness of allowing five nations to veto any resolution, we come as close as we can to an international "seal of approval." We all know, however, that the Security Council often finds itself unable to act and in those cases some other international body must play the role, as NATO did in Kosovo. The U.N. General Assembly can authorize military action under limited circumstances and can always state an opinion, which in and of itself can carry great weight. And the secretary general, chosen by the world body to be a global leader and charged by the U.N. Charter to "bring to the attention of the Security Council any matter which in his opinion may threaten the maintenance of international peace and security," has substantial moral authority by himself.

Will any of these mechanisms guarantee that intervention will be the wise or ethical thing to do in any specific instance? Of course not. The U.N. General Assembly, for example, has displayed at certain points in the past a deep-seated hostility to Israel, and one can imagine that, if it were left up to a simple majority of the world's countries, there are circumstances under which it might encourage military action against Israel or some other unpopular state that would be wholly indefensible. As the existentialist philosopher Soren Kierkegaard put it so resonantly, "the crowd is Untruth"; there is no guarantee that a decision by a multitude of parties will necessarily be better than a decision by an individual. But democracy is based on the premise that more often than not it will be, and what is surely true is that multilateralism provides a wider forum for debate and greater safeguards than the reckless abandon of one state or two acting alone.

Now we can see more clearly why the concept of an "international community" is so important and why attacks upon that construct by the likes of Condoleeza Rice, if not David Rieff, are so damaging. For if the "international community" is an "illusion," as Rice would have it, then there is no one to whom sovereign states are accountable, no plumb line by which to judge their actions, and no means by which to legitimize military intervention in the service of human rights or for any other purpose, for that matter. Every time the United States belittles the notion of an "international community," ignores or undermines its authority, be it in the name of fighting terrorism, countering weapons of mass destruction, or protecting human rights, it inflicts one more chink in the perilous effort to bring order and civility to a violent, fractured world. How can that possibly advance the cause of fighting terrorists who play on the very divisions it sows?

At the same time, to the extent the "international community" shirks its responsibilities, it does damage to its own credibility. That surely happened in 1994 in Rwanda. When the Security Council failed to act in the face of genocide, it was left to France, the only country willing to intervene, to take on the problem unilaterally. France did so belatedly but at least it did so, and the Security Council ultimately gave its blessing to the French initiative. The rule must therefore be something as ambiguous as "Intervention must be sanctioned by the international community except when, in the case of genocide or ethnic cleansing, that community is not willing to act."

But then that brings us to the question of the 2003 war in Iraq. There is good reason to believe that human rights violations were only a rationale of convenience for the war, but from a human rights point of view, Saddam Hussein, master of one of the world's most vicious regimes, utterly deserved to be removed from power. No one who cares about human rights could help but feel satisfaction at his toppling. To the extent that those who opposed the war failed to acknowledge the dastardliness of the Iraqi government and *to propose effective alternatives to war to relieve the Iraqi people of that burden,* they were indulging their ideology at the expense of others' suffering. If Hussein's brutality did not at least arguably warrant military intervention of some sort, the debate over that concept fails to be an interesting one.

The problem was that both the United States and its U.N. adversaries refused to genuinely engage in that debate. France and Germany declared military intervention out of bounds under any circumstances. Despite the simple option of giving the weapons inspectors a few more months to carry out their investigations, thereby assaying wider support for intervention eventually and lending it greater legitimacy, the United States made it clear almost from the beginning that it intended to damn the cruise missiles and go full steam ahead no matter what the international community thought. In the first instance, opponents of intervention appeared to care little for either the fate of the Iraqi people or protecting the world from massive casualties. In the latter, the United States, while it easily won the war, did enormous damage to the international framework within which human rights are cast and should be enforced, whether through military intervention or by other means. But then that, as I argued in chapter 2, may in part have been the very point.

Obviously, both the United States and the other key decision makers in the international community failed to take seriously the human rights calamity that Iraq had been for more than twenty years—the United States because it only "found religion" about human rights in Iraq when it suited larger purposes, and the anti-war segment of the international community because it seemed content to allow that calamity to continue unabated. One of the lessons to be learned from the circumstances leading up to the Iraq War is that, just as the United States may justifiably be chastised for asserting its unbridled sovereignty and thumbing its nose at the international community, so that community may be brought up short for failing to protect those being damaged by the exercise of another form of unbridled sovereignty in Iraq.

Interestingly enough, the United States has shown a willingness to sacrifice a measure of its own sovereignty in the economic field by its membership in the World Trade Organization (WTO). Under WTO rules, which the United States has agreed to abide by, if a dispute panel set up to hear a complaint about a country's trade practices rules against that country and its ruling is ignored, the offending country can be subjected to severe penalties, including stiff tariffs leveraged against its products. From the United States' point of view, this small sacrifice of sovereignty brings considerable dividends in the form of a more regularized international economy. What it fails to recognize is that the same could well be true when it comes to international relations.

Before September 11, 2001 the world was moving haltingly toward a new understanding of national sovereignty and its limits. There could be no better model of that than the European Union, with its common currency, porous borders, and agreement to subjugate some national laws (on human rights, for example) to regional authority. Fundamental to that model is the conviction that collective action is better than solitary, and that might requires the mandate of the neighborhood if its exercise is to be legitimate. The historian Robert Kagan has argued in his influential book *Of Paradise and Power* that the reason Europeans seek constraints on America through international legal mechanisms is simply because they are the weaker power trying to set limits to the stronger. But it was the victors in World Wars I and II, the strong, who established those international legal mechanisms in the first place—the League of Nations; the United Nations; the World Court; the Nuremberg and Tokyo trials and the current war crimes tribunals.[189]

To the extent that nations allow terrorists to use them as "blinds" for their activities or bases for operations, those nations may well legitimately be said to have sacrificed a portion of their sovereignty. But the war on terror makes it even more critical that intrusions upon that sovereignty come only with some form of international sanction, as the War in Afghanistan did, else we are left with such things as random unilateral interventions and unregulated assassinations of suspects. Actions such as those will inevitably damage any nation that tenders them in the eyes of the rest of the world. Prime Minister Mahathir Mohammad of Malaysia who, as we described earlier, was feted at the White House in May 2002 for his ardent support of the war on terror, despite his abysmal human rights record, had changed his tone markedly toward the United States less than one year later. Faced with United States threats to ignore the U.N. if it failed to authorize an invasion of Iraq, he observed, "You cannot trust someone who says, 'You will go along with other people, but if they don't want to follow, you will go on your own.'"[190]

Moreover, if the authority of the international community to ratify interventions is eroded, it will make it even harder than it already is to rally the world to stop the next genocide. As author Samantha Power has demonstrated, that worldwide will is already a weak one. When the United States seizes the war on terror as an excuse to reassert its disdain for the international human rights scaffolding, it is not only terrorists who triumph but *genocidiares* as well. If the genocide appears not directly related to terrorism, will we be even more inclined than ever to pay it no heed? If a Rwanda happened today, would we have learned any lessons from the past, or will we be too busy fighting terrorists to stop mass murder? Or might we come to see that massive human rights violations like genocide and ethnic cleansing can be the downfall of states and the incubator of the terrorist retinue?

Under extreme circumstances, state sovereignty may well appropriately give way to intervention, whether it be to pursue terrorists, end grave abuses, or deter the conflation of the two. But in the long run there is a far better solution to human rights crimes than military retaliation, and that is international justice. Here, too, however, the United States has played the spoiler.

• • •

The British hospital ship *Llandover Castle* was empty that dark night in the middle of World War I, empty of patients, as it plied its way across the North Atlantic returning home from Canada. But the German U-boat commander and his two junior officers did not know that when they fired their torpedoes at the ship; in fact they thought that it was carrying Air Force pilots. After the *Llandover Castle* went down, its few survivors clung desperately to three small lifeboats. The Germans, discovering that they had been mistaken about the pilots, were now faced with witnesses who could testify to their having fired on a medical vessel, so they sank the lifeboats, too. But one of the British sailors survived and testified against the three Germans in a German court. Two of them were convicted. The German government then promptly pardoned both. Indeed, of the 900 Germans identified by the Allies as war criminals in World War I and tried for their crimes before the German Supreme Court, 888 never stood trial. Of the twelve who did, six were acquitted and six convicted. And of the six convicted, all were pardoned within a few years.[191]

This was not the way it was meant to be. The Versailles Treaty, for all its faults, mandated the establishment of an international war crimes tribunal. But such a tribunal never came into existence. Britain and France favored it strongly, but the United States objected. Such a tribunal, said U.S. Secretary of State Robert Lansing, was a direct attack on state sovereignty and totally lacking in "precedent, precept, practice, or procedure."[192] It would take another world war before the principle of international accountability for war crimes would be put into practice.

The Nuremberg and Tokyo trials, as well as, more recently, the war crimes tribunals for Rwanda and the former Yugoslavia, have been the vehicles for such accountability. The United States has been a key supporter of them all. Each of them has advanced the notion that sovereignty is no protector of barbarism and "just following orders" no excuse for human rights crimes. But now comes the International Criminal Court (ICC), whose statute entered into force on July 1, 2002 a permanent court in contrast to the *ad hoc* bodies referred to above, charged with bringing to justice those accused of genocide, war crimes, and crimes against humanity; and the United States has gone all weak in the knees. Worse than that, the Bush administration has "unsigned" the ICC treaty to which President Bill Clinton had affixed his signature, has threatened countries that support the ICC, and has sought exemption from prosecution for any U.S. troops who might be a part of peacekeeping operations overseas.

And what has prompted such hostility? The fear that American soldiers and, even more alarmingly, American political leaders, might be subject to capricious prosecution by a rogue prosecutor or judges intent on punishing the world's only superpower. This despite the provision in the ICC's charter (it's called "complementarity") that stipulates that anyone charged with a crime falling within the ICC's jurisdiction may be tried first in his or her home country's courts and, as long as the process is conducted in good faith, the judgment of that domestic court will stand. It is hard to avoid the suspicion that the United States is invoking Robert Lansing's state sovereignty defense on behalf of only one state—itself. And it is a telling paradox that, in its violation of international standards regarding the treatment of foreign nationals, its refusal to fully comply with the Geneva Conventions as they apply to prisoners at Guantanamo Bay, and its invocation of the category "unlawful combatant" to describe American citizens whom it would deprive of due process, the United States is modeling that very capriciousness it claims to expect from the ICC.

If instead of resisting the creation of an international structure of accountability before which the worst human rights violators could be brought, the United States supported this groundbreaking effort, it would pay rich dividends. As things stand now, universal jurisdiction can be invoked by any prosecutor of any country that recognizes that principle for the purposes of questioning or bringing a case against any political or military figure, such as the Spanish judge Baltazar Garzon did with Augusto Pinochet in 1999. Such *ad hoc* prosecutions may well grow in the future and that may be all to the good. The ICC will, after all, only be able to prosecute a limited number of cases and some countries may opt to prosecute others themselves. But, far from contributing to unjustified legal harassment, a standing international court could systematize the most important prosecutions, lend them legitimacy, and provide a model of conduct and responsibility for similar national endeavors.

Were the United States to ratify the court, it would then be in a position to work to amend the ICC's rules of procedure, as necessary, participate in the selection of judges and prosecutors, and watch over the court's development. Whether the ICC exists or not, American leaders are legally vulnerable to the whims of national prosecutors invoking universal jurisdiction all over the world. By supporting the ICC, we institutionalize the principle of complementarity for countries like our own which have fully functioning judicial systems and we provide a court of last resort for those less developed countries whose own judicial systems are unlikely to be able to handle prosecutions of the world's worst tyrants.

Even more important, a U.S.-backed ICC would send a powerful message to would-be miscreants around the world: you will pay legal consequences if you commit the most dastardly crimes. I don't mean for a second that the court is a panacea, any more than the existence of any criminal justice system, no matter how effective, guarantees an end to crime. But imagine how different our world would be today if Augusto Pinochet, Pol Pot, Idi Amin, and "Baby Doc" Duvalier had all been hauled before an international court, convicted of human rights crimes, and punished for them, instead of allowed, as they were and have been, to live out their lives in peace? How can we possibly know that such consistent justice would have had no effect upon Slobodan Milosovic, Saddam Hussein, or the *genocidiaires* of Rwanda? It is at least arguable that one or more of them would have thought twice about committing their crimes if they had seen their predecessors in infamy behind bars.

Then, too, the availability of a reliable mechanism for administering international justice would help resolve one of the thorniest dilemmas the world frequently faces: namely, whether a tyrant should be offered safe exile or amnesty in exchange for giving up power peacefully and saving the toll of war. In the months leading up to the Iraq War, the United States cited Saddam Hussein's atrocious record of torture and executions as one of the rationales for taking military action against him. But then we also let it be known that if the "Butcher of Baghdad" were to opt for exile, we would not try to stop him. Such leniency raises a question as to how serious America's concern for Saddam's human rights record could be if we were prepared to see him go scot-free. On the other hand, if his exile had averted a war and the subsequent suffering of the Iraqi people, who had already paid a great price at the hands of their own government, might safe passage not have been the lesser of two evils? The only reason we are faced with this Hobson's choice is because the world has refused for centuries to hold tyrants to systematic legal account. Absent a functioning system of truly global justice, war seems far too often like the only option. But with such a system, the message to would-be Saddams will be quite clear: "There no longer is any place where a human rights offender like you can go and be confident he will not face the long arm of retribution, so you had better think twice before putting yourself in a position of having to choose between prosecution or annihilation."

The ICC, as currently constituted, may be of only limited assistance when it comes to prosecuting terrorists. The court cannot address crimes committed before it came into existence (e.g., the events of September 11, 2001) and it can only prosecute individuals from countries that have ratified the treaty. But in seven years, when the first review conference of the Court takes place, crimes of terrorism could well be added to its mandate and even before then, were other crimes on the scale of 9/11 to occur, God forbid, they might well fall under the court's current jurisdiction as crimes against humanity. In any case, a strong ICC will constitute an unprecedented affirmation of global, in addition to national, justice. As the philosopher Peter Singer has observed, that can have profound implications in the struggle against terrorism:

> Terrorism has made our world an integrated community in a new and frightening way. Not merely the activities of our neighbors, but those of the inhabitants of the most remote mountain valleys of the farthest-flung countries of our planet, have become our business. We need to extend the reach of criminal law there and to have the means to bring terrorists to justice without declaring war on an entire country in order to do so.[193]

Terrorism must be fought both militarily and criminally. At the moment, the criminal justice systems that are fighting it are all national in scope. To this point the United States has chosen to utilize only its own courts to prosecute terrorist suspects. But how much more powerful it would be if those accused of terrorism were subjected to *international* censure? How much more difficult it would be for anyone to claim that convictions were set up or tainted by anti-Islamic sentiment if the prosecutors and judges were not just Americans but Danes and Kazakhs and Nigerians and Jordanians and Pakistanis as well? The United States is hardly likely to permit the Osama bin Ladens of the world to be tried before some sort of international tribunal if it is not even willing to support the ICC. And that, once again, is unfortunate because it signals, as does our opposition to the ICC itself, an utter disdain for multilateral institutions, institutions which, if allowed to flourish, could be one of the most promising means to create a more secure world.

The Yoruba tribe of Africa has a myth as to how the world was populated by the multitude of tribes and nations we find today. Before there were any people in the world, they say, Many-Worm (who lived deep inside the soil) began to split apart into separate segments. Each of these segments grew hands and feet and gradually they made their way to the surface of the earth. When the young son of the One Great God heard them coming, he was delighted and prepared to welcome them. He painted his face, shook his rattle furiously and danced up and down for joy. When Many-Worm's segments finally reached the surface and encountered all this ruckus, they were scared to death and quickly slithered back into the ground. So the young son of the One Great God changed his tack. This time he shook his rattle softly, sang a soothing song and called out this message to the worm-people: "Come out! Come out to the bright new land. Each one of you can do one good thing and still you can hold hands." And with that the worm-people made their way to the surface, blinked at the sunlight and decided to stay. "This place looks good," they said. "It is a bright new land in which every one of us can do one good thing and still we can hold hands."

There are 191 nations in the world in which 6,170 languages are spoken.[194] The world is a multitextured, many segmented place, and it is likely to stay that way. That is by no means all bad—every one of those segments could do at least one good thing, if only they would.

But it is also a place recognizing slowly but inexorably that its very survival depends upon its willingness in some measure to hold hands. That is surely true when it comes to human rights but also when it comes to health, environmental safety, and a more equitable distribution of wealth. It is also true when it comes to combating terrorism. If any enterprise required the world's responsible states to sacrifice just a bit of their sovereignty in order to join hands against those who would spread fear upon the waters, it is that one.

The Bush administration has even given voice to this truism. Under Secretary of Defense for Policy Douglas Feith has said, "I think that we may be on our way to creating a new international way of thinking, a new international norm, about terrorism. . . . Our goal is to make terrorism like piracy, the slave trade, or genocide in the minds of the people around the world. It is to delegitimate terrorism as an activity."[195] But far from recognizing its interdependence with other countries in practice, the United States seems to have drawn from the threat of terrorism the lesson that it must rely more and more on its own stubborn strength alone. That is a tragic miscalculation—exceeded perhaps only by the conclusion that in the fight against terrorism, all is permitted—including torture.

CHAPTER 7

The Ticklish Case of a Ticking Bomb:

Is Torture Ever Justified?

Do not think only of what you wish to gain but think too of what you will lose to gain it—the sacrifice of so much that is good, the dangers and disasters of what you will incur.[196]

Erasmus

When it comes to torture, simple is often best. Ants like molasses. That is why those fighting for Filipino independence at the turn of the twentieth century smeared the heads of their American prisoners with it before burying them alive up to their necks. The Americans occupying the Philippines at the time got their revenge, however. They used the infamous "water cure," a bamboo tube stuck down the subject's throat through which enormous quantities of water, the filthier the better, were poured. The mujahideen in Afghanistan were known to tie their prisoners to corpses and let the "package" lie in the sun for days on end. Sticks and truncheons, particularly when used to beat the most vulnerable parts of the body, like the soles of the feet, are still the most common instruments of choice for torturers, but one reason electroshock weapons, such as stun guns, have become more and more popular around the world, including in the United States, is because they leave no marks. One push of the button. No fuss, no mess.

Common as torture is (Amnesty International has documented the torture or ill treatment of prisoners in at least 130 countries), no country has ever acknowledged that its use is official policy. Israel came closest when, for awhile, it authorized its interrogators to use "moderate physical pressure" on prisoners, which turned out to include violent shaking of the head and holding prisoners for long periods in awkward positions. But the Israeli Supreme Court eventually outlawed such force, although Israel had always denied that "moderate physical pressure" constituted torture, anyway.

Indeed, the practice is banned by one human rights convention after another, beginning with the Universal Declaration of Human Rights and including the International Covenant on Civil and Political Rights (ICCPR). The Convention against Torture and Other Cruel, Inhuman, and Degrading Treatment or Punishment (CAT) was adopted by the U.N. General Assembly in 1984 and has been ratified by 129 countries, including the United States in 1994. It defines torture as "any act by which severe pain or suffering, whether physical or mental, is intentionally inflicted by or at the instigation of a public official on a person for such purposes as obtaining information . . . or confession," and the convention makes clear that "no exceptional circumstances whatsoever, whether a state of war or a threat of war, internal political instability, or any other public emergency may be invoked as a justification for torture."[197] Torture is, in other words, one of those nonderogable rights that are prohibited absolutely under all circumstances. That is one reason why, under international law, torturers are considered *hostis humani generis*, enemies of all humanity, and why all countries have jurisdiction to prosecute them, regardless of where the torture took place.

Despite this universal prohibition, the case for using torture under certain circumstances has begun to receive a more and more respectable hearing since September 11, 2001 and not just in countries that have rarely displayed many scruples about the question. Writing in *Newsweek* shortly after the attacks, for example, Jonathan Alter, a self-identified liberal columnist, admitted that his "thoughts [were] turning to . . . torture" and that, while "we can't legalize physical torture . . . , we need to keep an open mind about certain measures to fight terrorism . . . we'll have to think about transferring some suspects to our less squeamish allies, even if that's hypocritical."[198] In January 2002 Bruce Hoffman, director of the Washington office of RAND, contributed a piece to *The Atlantic Monthly* called "A Nasty Business," in which he reassured readers that he was "never bidden to condone, much less advocate, torture," but then went on to say that "I recall the ruthless enemy that America faces and I wonder about the lengths to which we may yet have to go to vanquish him."[199] The most forthright voice urging a reexamination of our aversion to torture, however, belongs to Professor Alan Dershowitz of Harvard Law School, a longtime champion of civil liberties, who came up with the idea of court-sanctioned "torture warrants" to legitimize behavior he thought inevitable anyhow.[200]

These gentlemen did not have to wait long to see their speculative notions take on the apparent raiment of reality. As early as October 2001, the *Washington Post* reported that American officials were frustrated by the silence of jailed Al Qaeda suspects and might have to resort to "pressure tactics" or extradition to countries "where security services . . . resort to torture."[201] Over the next year or so, as growing numbers of terrorist suspects fell into American hands, reports began to leak out that the United States had opted for exactly that. The *Christian Science Monitor* claimed in July 2002 that the United States was shipping suspects to Egypt, Syria, and Jordan—countries that "use torture, which . . . extracts information more quickly than more benign interrogation methods"[202] and in December 2002 the *Post* broke a major story describing "stress and duress" techniques employed at the U.S.-occupied Bagram Air Base in Afghanistan. "Stress and duress" included such things as keeping black-hooded prisoners standing or kneeling for hours, forcing them to maintain "awkward, painful positions," and depriving them of sleep with a twenty-four hour bombardment of light. "If you don't violate someone's human rights some of the time," one official said, "you probably aren't doing your job." The *Post* story also confirmed the earlier reports that prisoners were being transferred or "rendered" to countries in which torture was a common interrogatory practice. "We don't kick the [expletive] out of them," another official was quoted as saying. "We send them to other countries so that they can kick the [expletive] out of them."[203]

A few months later the *New York Times* elaborated, describing what "senior American officials" called "acceptable techniques like sleep and light deprivation and the temporary withholding of food, water, access to sunlight, and medical attention."[204] Two detainees in U.S. custody at Bagram Air Base died of "blunt force injuries" in what a military pathologist listed as homicides and, while those deaths are the subject of an investigation, most of these reports of torture were met initially with perfunctory denials from the Bush administration.[205] President Bush himself assured the U.N. High Commissioner for Human Rights that the "U.S. has not and will not use torture in interrogating prisoners" but said nothing about "acceptable techniques" such as those described by the *Times*, which the U.S.A. may not regard as torture, and nothing about the transfer of prisoners to other countries.[206] Was it possible that the United States was employing tactics the use of which it had long denounced around the globe and hardly being apologetic about it?[207] Nor was there much of an outcry from the American people. But then in October 2001, 45 percent of Americans had told pollsters that they approved of "the torture of known terrorists if they know details about future terrorist attacks."[208] Obviously, Americans' attitudes toward their government's intentional use of brutality had changed mightily.

That was because Americans were frightened and the government had led them to believe that the application of "stress and duress" was one important way it could help to make them safer. It was not, presumably, that the suspects were being tortured for gratuitous or sadistic reasons or to make a political point, or for revenge or to set an example that would discourage other terrorists from following the terrorist path—all motivations that have prompted other instances of torture around the world. It was purely, or so American officials claimed, to extract intelligence in order to ward off future attacks.

The situation, then, was a variation on the classic philosophical scenario—the case of the ticking bomb. Dershowitz had premised his arguments for torture warrants on the same hypothetical: suppose the authorities are holding a suspect who knows where a ticking bomb is located, a bomb that will kill hundreds or thousands of people if it explodes. Would they be justified in torturing the suspect to procure the information and thereby save innocent lives? Virtually every "introduction to ethics" class takes up the same question, a question that holds enormous fascination, command, and now perhaps direct relevance for large numbers of people. Indeed, if we human rights advocates cannot respond adequately to this challenge, the hope that we can persuade governments to stop using torture and citizens to stop encouraging them will be utterly futile. It is therefore more than worthwhile to meet the challenge head-on.

• • •

Frank Snepp was the C.I.A.'s Chief Strategy Analyst in Vietnam during the Vietnam War. In a 1977 book about the war, he describes a technique for interrogation taught him by the chief C.I.A. officer in My Tho that was guaranteed to "break a prisoner in less than forty-eight hours." It was called, ironically in light of today's circumstances, the "Arabic method," and it was simple: "undress the subject, bandage his eyes, tie him to an armless, straight-backed chair, then let him sit—and sit."

> Eventually, after three or four hours, he loses all sense of orientation ("returns to the womb"). Then you begin questioning him, softly and soothingly at half-hour intervals, a voice out of the gloom. Guaranteed: he'll be eating out of your hand by the following morning.[209]

And there will be no blood on your hands. But is such a technique acceptable? Is it torture? Or at least "cruel, inhuman, and degrading treatment"? Those of us who care about human rights need to be quick to admit that gaining information from prisoners is critically important. It can help save lives, and that is in large measure what our work is about. Nor do prisoners need to be treated like house guests. But they must also not be denied the rudiments of civilized life—no matter how uncivilized their own behavior may have been.

The truth is that what is acceptable and unacceptable from a human rights standpoint is not always 100 percent clear. Reports have it that the United States has resorted to deception (it's called "false flag" operations) in its questioning of Al Qaeda suspects, putting up signs in interrogation rooms that lead them to believe they are in a New York City police station, for example. Women have been chosen to do the questioning of Muslim men to take advantage of cultural prejudices. The hours between meals have been altered to induce time disorientation. These types of techniques probably do not violate international strictures. But forcing suspects to kneel for hours in uncomfortable positions in extreme heat or cold, shackling their hands to the ceiling and feet to the floor for prolonged periods and depriving them of food, water, and medical attention—all these certainly do.

Are these instances of torture or "cruel, inhuman, and degrading treatment"? The stipulation that torture must entail "severe pain and suffering, whether physical or mental" means that there will be an element of subjectivity in the judgment as to when "cruel, inhuman, and degrading treatment" shades into torture and even what is cruel and degrading in the first place. The European Court of Human Rights found in 1978, for example, in a case concerning British treatment of prisoners suspected of being members of the Irish Republican Army that, while it was not "torture" to force them to stand spread-eagled against a wall for hours or be deprived of sleep, it *was* "inhuman and degrading" treatment and therefore a breach of the European Convention on Human Rights.[210] Ultimately, it is up to the courts to decide practice by practice, but for a human rights–respecting nation, anything that even approaches such mistreatment ought to be avoided. The bottom line is that, whether it be torture or cruel, inhuman, and degrading treatment, it is abhorrent and a violation of international law. And that is true whether a country's own agents are inflicting the pain or making it possible for the agents of other nations to do so.[211]

Be this as it may, there is much that is tempting in the "ticking bomb" argument, the notion that the infliction of suffering upon one person, particularly suffering that stops short of causing that person's death, is a fair trade-off to save the lives of hundreds of others. And in a strict, if abstract, utilitarian calculus, that is true. But real life is neither abstract nor strict, and even if we limit ourselves to a cold cost-benefit analysis, the long-term consequences of violating others' human rights are rarely clear ahead of time.

Take the Philippines at the turn of the last century and the torture described at the outset of this chapter. In one sense the victims of the Americans' "water cure" were the lucky ones. "I want no prisoners," demanded American Gen. Jacob Smith of his soldiers. "I wish you to kill and burn, the more you kill and burn the better it will please me."[212] Smith got his wish and the United States got the Philippines, maintaining a military presence until shortly after our allied strong-man, Ferdinand Marcos, and his abusive regime fell in 1986.

But Filipinos have long memories and when, in 2002–03, the United States wanted to send troops to the Philippines to fight the terrorist group Abu Sayyaf, the proposal met with enormous resist-ance from the local population. Not because of our close association with the hated Marcos. It was "the experience a century ago of American soldiers conducting bloody insurgency campaigns" that stoked feelings of mistrust and alienation, said one observer.[213] Stories of torture and death inflicted upon the indigenous people by the American military had been passed on from one generation to the next until they had taken on "mythical proportions."[214] All those long-ago water cures threatened to wash away the Americans' abil-ity to stop terrorism today.

Proponents of ticking bomb torture try to convince us that the calculation is straightforward: torture one terrorist; save 100 people. But that assumes that there are no further detrimental conse-quences once the victims of the bombing are saved—no retaliatory strikes, for example, by the torture victim's comrades to pay back the inhumanity done their brother. If that happens, the math may quickly change: 100 people saved today; 1,000 killed tomorrow.

The French were notorious for using torture against the National Liberation Front (FLN) during the Algerian war.[215] Bruce Hoffman admits that the "sheer brutality" of their torture "alienated the native Algerian Muslim community. Hitherto mostly passive or apathetic, that community was now driven into the arms of the FLN, swelling the organization's ranks and increasing its popular support."[216] If Israel's experience is any guide, the fact that the authorities may be able to prevent one deadly incident through torture or ill treatment of a suspect is no guarantee of an end to the cycle of violence. Indeed, such treatment may even help perpetuate it. As Dr. Ruchamas Marton, the founder of Israel's Physicians for Human Rights puts it, those subjected to torture "are broken after the experience. . . . Their families . . . want to take revenge."[217] Or they themselves do. One Palestinian teenager tortured at the Gush Etzion police station in 2001 declared that, though he had been arrested for throwing stones at settlers' cars, the degradation he had experienced in prison had made him want to become a suicide bomber.[218]

But *is* torture an effective means of gaining information to stop ticking bombs in the first place? It seems more than passing strange that, though the ticking bomb scenario has been used for decades to justify torture, its defenders rarely cite verifiable cases from real life that mirrors its conditions. Israeli authorities, for example, have often made the general assertion that their interrogation practices have saved lives, but they fail to detail specific examples. The case of Abdul Hakim Murad, a convicted terrorist plotter tortured by Filipino authorities, is sometimes referenced because the information he provided foiled a plot to crash nearly a dozen U.S. airliners into the Pacific.[219] And of course Guy Fawkes, of Gunpowder Plot fame, was stretched on the rack in the Tower of London in 1605 until he gave up the names of his accomplices. But the number of true, confirmed ticking bomb cases is infinitesimal, certainly in comparison to the number of innocent people who have been tortured around the world.

Perhaps, upon reflection, however, the absence of verifiable cases is not so strange. For what the ticking bomb case asks us to believe is that the authorities know that a bomb has been planted somewhere, know it is about to go off, know that the suspect in their custody has the information they need to stop it, know that the suspect will yield that information accurately in a matter of minutes if subjected to torture, and know that there is no other way to obtain it. The scenario asks us to believe, in other words, that the authorities have all the information that authorities dealing with a crisis *never* have.

Even aficionados of ticking bomb torture agree that its use can only be justified as a last resort applicable to those we know to a moral certainty are guilty and possess the information we seek. Those 45 percent of Americans who reported in October 2001 that they approved of torture were approving of the "torture of *known terrorists* if the terrorists *know details* about future terrorist attacks [emphasis added]." But how do we know for sure who is a "known terrorist" or that they "know details"? Isn't that exactly what the torture is presumably designed to find out? The reason torture is such a risky proposition is exactly because it is so *difficult* to tell ahead of time who is a terrorist and who is not; who has the information and who does not; who will give the information accurately and who will deceive; who will respond to torture and who will endure it as a religious discipline.

What if there is only a 50 percent chance the suspect has the information we seek? Is torture justified then? What if it is only a 10 percent chance?[220] The fact is that many people suspected of being terrorists turn out not to be, as our experience with the 1,100-some detainees taken into custody after September 11 has proved so well. What if those innocent people had been manhandled even more than they were? What more surefire way could we imagine to foster resentment in the communities from which they came—the very communities whose citizens are potentially the source of exactly the kind of inside information about terrorist operatives that we need to stop terrorism in the first place?

Many experts on interrogation believe that torture is one of the *least* effective ways to gain accurate information from suspects. A 1963 C.I.A. training manual observed that "interrogatees who have withstood pain are more difficult to handle by other methods. The effect has not been to repress the subject but to restore his confidence and maturity."[221] On the other hand, if the torture victim "cracks," he is likely to say anything to make the pain stop. Insists Eric Haney, a former interrogator for the United States Army, "Torture just makes the person tell you what they think that you want to know so you'll stop hurting them." The French were unabashed in their employment of torture in Algeria, even though the names of the terrorists yielded up by its victims were, as they themselves later admitted, "not always necessarily the right name."[222] Abdul Hakim Murad, the terrorist who talked in the Philippines, provided information about the airliners, but he also claimed to be responsible for the bombing of the Federal building in Oklahoma City.[223] Many of the false code orange terrorist alerts the United States has experienced in the past two years have been prompted by bad information passed on by detainees under harsh questioning.[224]

Other approaches are generally more effective. Art Hulnick, a former C.I.A. officer, who interviewed North Korean prisoners after the Korean War, reported that prisoners taken into custody by American troops and treated humanely were much more forthcoming, over time, than those held by the South Koreans and tortured.[225] The F.B.I. teaches thirty techniques to make suspects talk without crossing the line into mistreatment—from inducing boasts to making false promises.[226] Even Abdul Hakim Murad "spilled the beans" not as a result of torture itself but after Philippine intelligence officials pretended they were agents from Israel's Mossad to which, they said, Hakim was being turned over.[227]

The secret for "human intelligence collectors," as the questioners are now called, is to establish "positive control." Retired Army Maj. Gen. Bill Nash describes that as "imposing on [prisoners] a psychological sense of isolation, domination, and futility, and trying to establish the conditions by which you can then reward them for information, as opposed to punish them."[228] In fact, one of the reasons the U.S. government objected to allowing American citizen

Jose Padilla, the so-called dirty bomber, to see a lawyer was because
it was afraid a lawyer's intrusion would harm "the military's efforts to
develop a relationship of trust and dependency that is essential to
effective interrogation."[229] As Christopher Whitcomb, a former
F.B.I. interrogation instructor, put it:

> Interrogation is an art form, not a street fight. It is built on
> guile, perseverance, and a keen understanding of how people
> respond to need. People will tell you anything if you present
> the questions in the proper context. You simply have to find
> the right way to ask.[230]

"Everybody talks eventually," says former F.B.I. agent Rick
Smith. "It's just a matter of time."[231]

But time is what ticking bomb advocates claim not to have. And yet
the truth is that the stereotypical ticking bomb scenario—ten minutes
to extract information needed to save lives—is almost entirely a fiction.
Would torture be justified if the bomb were to go off in ten hours?
How about ten days? Or ten months? The Al Qaeda suspects being
mistreated by the United States and its allies today do not apparently
possess information about events that are about to happen in ten minutes, for, if they did, even larger numbers of Americans would by now
be dead. The United States is clearly not limiting its torture to ticking
bombers. But then, as the Israeli High Court found to its chagrin,
"moderate physical pressure" to obtain intelligence not only tended to
morph into unqualified torture but was gradually applied to more and
more people—not just the ticking bomb terrorists.

And then there is another slippery slope. For if it is legitimate to
torture a terrorist to obtain crucial information to save hundreds of
lives, is it also morally defensible to torture the terrorist's wife or
children? How about his aged mother? How about his whole family?
Where do we stop? At what point do we truly give up our souls?

Given all these drawbacks to torture, is there any way to salvage its "respectability" in the face of a ticking bomb? Alan Dershowitz thinks there is. Dershowitz contends that, whether we like it or not, officials confronted with a ticking bomb would inevitably resort to torture and, what's more, the vast majority of us would want them to. But because any officer who did so might be subject to prosecution, despite the availability of the common law defense that the commission of a crime may be justified if it is necessary to prevent a greater evil, the onus of responsibility should not be left on the individual official. Instead, the authorities should apply to a court for a "torture warrant," similar to a search warrant, so that the courts must bear the burden of authorizing torture or the consequences of failing to do so. This is also the best way, he suggests, to limit its application. Dershowitz has assured us that "the suspect [in such cases] would be given immunity from prosecution based on information elicited by torture" and that "the warrant would limit the torture to nonlethal means, such as sterile needles being inserted beneath the nails to cause excruciating pain without endangering life."[232] But will a warrant make torture right?

To see the shoals upon which the "torture warrant" flounders, consider this. There is no doubt that, despite official efforts to eradicate it, police brutality is practiced in many U.S. jurisdictions and probably always will be. Some police officers will claim, in their more candid moments, that the use of excessive force is often the only way to protect the lives of officers and the general public. Why ought the police not be able, therefore, to apply for "brutality warrants" in specialized cases? Why ought police officers who believe that a little shaving of the truth on the witness stand is worth sending a bunch of drug pushers to prison, thus protecting hundreds of youngsters from a life of drugs and crime, not be able to seek "testilying warrants"? Why ought correctional officers who argue that allowing dominant male prisoners to rape other prisoners helps preserve order among thugs and thus protects the lives of guards—

why ought such officers not be allowed to seek "warrants to tolerate prisoner rape" in particularly dangerous situations? The answer in all cases is the same: because the act itself (brutalizing citizens, committing perjury, facilitating rape) is itself abhorrent and illegal. Dershowitz's analogy to search warrants fails because, while a particular search may itself be illegal, the act of searching is not *ipso facto* unethical or a crime. For a society to start providing its imprimatur to criminal acts because they are common or may appear to provide a shortcut to admirable ends is an invitation to chaos.

Moreover, Dershowitz's hypothetical application of the torture warrant proposal to the events of September 11 shows exactly what is wrong with it. "Had law enforcement officials arrested terrorists boarding one of the [September 11] airplanes and learned that other planes, then airborne, were headed toward unknown occupied buildings," Dershowitz proposes, "there would have been an understandable incentive to torture those terrorists in order to learn the identity of the buildings and evacuate them."[233] But this assumes that those law enforcement officials would have had time in the hour and a half or so between the boarding of the planes and the impact on their targets to (1) take the suspects into custody; (2) ascertain with enough certainty to warrant torture that the suspects were (a) terrorists who (b) had the needed information in their possession; (3) apply to a judge for a torture warrant and make the case for one; (4) inflict torture sufficient to retrieve the necessary facts; (5) evaluate the validity of those facts in order to be assured that no innocent plane would be identified and blown out of the sky; and (6) take the steps required to stop or mitigate the terrorist act. Perhaps after John Ashcroft has been attorney general another few years, law enforcement will have learned to cut enough corners of the legal niceties to accomplish this feat, but at the moment, given all the bureaucratic infighting at the new Department of Homeland Security, it seems unlikely.

Trying to legitimize torture through the issuing of warrants will hardly make the practice scarcer, as Dershowitz would like, but to institutionalize it as a respectable option. Of course some authorities may utilize torture under some circumstances just as others choose to take bribes. The question is, "What is the best way to eradicate these practices?" By regulating them or outlawing them and enforcing the law? That an evil seems pervasive or even (at the moment) inevitable is no reason to grant it official approval. We tried that when it came to slavery and the result was the Civil War. Had we adopted Professor Dershowitz's approach to child labor, American ten-year olds would still be sweating in shops.

Dershowitz's idea of torture warrants is a nonstarter though it *is* comforting to know that, if the professor's plan is ever implemented, the needles will be sterile.

• • •

In 1999 the United States issued its required report to the United Nations Committee Against Torture. "Torture is prohibited by law throughout the United States," that report said.

> It is categorically denounced as a matter of policy and as a tool of state authority. Every act constituting torture under the [Convention Against Torture] constitutes a criminal offense under the law of the United States. No official of the government . . . , civilian or military, is authorized to commit or to instruct anyone else to commit torture. Nor may any official condone or tolerate torture in any form. No exceptional circumstances may be invoked as a justification of torture.[234]

You can't get much more unequivocal than that.

It doesn't take much imagination to see, then, how quickly the use of torture would diminish the credibility of a struggle against terrorism that is being fought in the name of defending American values and the rule of law. How many people would need to be tortured before our allies threw up their hands in disgust and our adversaries started celebrating their moral victory? And what could we possibly do that would be more likely to increase the possibility that American service men and women who fall into the hands of our adversaries may themselves be subject to such treatment? On what conceivable grounds could we plead for their protection from it?

It is sad that a nation that has always prided itself on its defense of the humane should now find itself the perpetrator of the repugnant. But it is not all that surprising. In order to inflict torture, you must on some emotional level understand your victim to be subhuman and therefore not eligible to claim *human* rights. "Barbarians," Vice President Cheney's word, does nicely. The irony is that torture stains the torturer almost as much as it wounds his victim. The tragedy is that we are corroding our society even as we try to save it. "Barbarian." "Torturer." Two different words with much in common. Two words to ponder.

PART III RECONSTRUCTION

CHAPTER 8 Striking the Rights Balance:

Security, Liberty, and the Challenge of a New World

Oh Lord, how beautiful must have been the faces trampled in the dust.

Urdu poem

By this point, I expect that those who regard human rights as largely expendable in the face of threats to national security will, if they have gotten this far, not be happy with this book. But now it is time to irritate supporters of human rights as well. To insist that all rights must still be fully protected under all circumstances, even the threat of terrorism, will simply not wash anymore. September 11 may not have "changed everything," but it certainly changed some things and, if we in the human rights community fail to recognize that we are living in a new world, if we are unwilling to think about rights in new ways, we end up being righteous at the expense of being relevant. If, in other words, we try to hold the old line everywhere, we will not be able to hold a new one anywhere—even in such fundamental places as providing legal counsel to prisoners or stopping torture of suspects.

The truth is that respecting human rights in day-to-day life is not always an exact science. Those who have to protect innocent lives rather than merely talk about doing so face real dilemmas that are not easily resolved. Here are some of the quandaries:

- If there is good reason to believe that the New York City subway system or Minnesota's Mall of America might be prime targets for terrorist attack, does it really make sense to object in the name of privacy rights to the installation of surveillance cameras, particularly if the evidence obtained can only be used for a limited set of purposes?

- "If you can make Jell-O, you can wipe out cities. Enjoy!" reads a book called *Scientific Principles of Improvised Warfare* that describes where to find anthrax spores and how to turn them into an aerosol spray. This is but one of dozens of "self-help" books available at gun shows and through the Internet that inform would-be terrorists, foreign or domestic, how to manufacture and disseminate weapons of mass destruction (WMD). If we can set legitimate limits to the publication of government secrets about nuclear weapons, for example, or restrict access to child pornography, might there not be a way to prevent books like these from falling into the wrong hands without doing untold damage to our civil liberties?

- Given that every American has a social security number and files taxes, and many have drivers' licenses, the government already has a host of information on every one of us. Will a national identification card coded electronically to prevent falsification of identity necessarily be so great an additional intrusion into our private lives, or are there ways to limit its use in an acceptable fashion?

- Profiling by every conceivable category (race, gender, age, income, household location, educational level) is common for purposes of marketing products. The International Covenant on Civil and Political Rights outlaws discrimination that is based *solely* on certain categories, like religion or social origin. Are there not reasonable forms of profiling that transcend race, religion, and ethnicity by means of which authorities can narrow the field of those who might carry a bomb onto a plane or plant a toxin in a water system?

- If democratic elections bring a radical Islamist government to power in Pakistan and that government begins to make nuclear weapons available to Al Qaeda, would we conclude that democracy in Pakistan was still preferable to military rule?

- If Saudi Arabia offers to limit its financial support for terrorist networks and, while respecting due process, extradite terrorist suspects to the United States to stand trial, ought we temper our criticism of the kingdom's human rights record long enough to guarantee their cooperation?

- While all armies or police forces can be perpetrators of human rights violations, including, as we have seen in the past, those flying the flag of the U.N., might it be an acceptable risk to run to create a U.N. standing army or police force if such a force could control regional conflicts, thereby saving lives and denying safe havens to terrorists?

There are not always easy answers, but too often those who support human rights and civil liberties have been unwilling even to grapple with the questions. That is in part because those of us in the advocacy community are primarily cheerleaders for our cause rather than policy makers for our government.

I do not use the term "cheerleader" disparagingly. I mean that a major part of our role is to inspire public debate, form public opinion, bring constituent pressure to bear upon decision makers—in short, to exercise our democratic prerogatives—and thereby try to sway government. Some organizations also file litigation and draft legislation, but most advocacy groups are principally that—advocates for a particular point of view. Faced as they are by stolid opponents only too eager to poke holes in their arguments, they find it inconvenient to give public voice to their own doubts or the ambiguities of their own position. Oberlin College, from which I graduated, was by no means a football giant. One afternoon, when we trailed Ohio Wesleyan by some forty-three points, the cheerleading squad led the Oberlin minions in chanting, "You may lead by forty-three but we have higher SATs." It would be rare to find a social justice organization willing to give similar acknowledgment to both the strengths *and* weaknesses of its perspective. Indeed, if you believe that truth emerges from the clash of vividly stated alternatives, you would not want advocacy groups to do anything but argue as vociferously as they can for their side of the story.

The danger is, however, that raucous cheers can transmogrify so easily into rigid ideologies, and when that happens public officials, who either have to save lives or face the consequences, may quite understandably stop listening. In the face of terror without end, it is not good enough just to tell authorities all they are doing wrong. It is incumbent upon critics to try to help those wielding the power do so in a constructive, effective fashion. One place to start is by calling "terror" terror.

• • •

"Religious believers convinced that flat tires were the key to salvation deflated tires on scores of buses and cars yesterday, paralyzing traffic throughout the city [of Manila]." So read an Associated Press news story almost a decade ago that described "terrified motorists" abandoning their vehicles and fleeing for safety. When asked why they had liberated the air from so many tires, one of the believers explained, "This is God's order to let out air. Air is from God. This is the solution to the crisis in our country."[235] Period. Clear enough.

But were the shenanigans in Manila the acts of terrorists? Here is the United States government's statutory definition of terrorism: "Premeditated, politically motivated violence perpetrated against noncombatant targets by sub national groups or clandestine agents, usually intended to influence an audience."[236] Though we don't know enough details of the Manila incident to say for certain, it appears to come close to meeting that definition. Today I suspect the government would be happy to include "religiously motivated" violence in its description, in addition to "politically," but, inasmuch as the believers saw the release of air as "the solution to the crisis in [their] country," perhaps political motivations are apparent as well. I feel fairly confident that if this incident were repeated today, some Filipino official, newscaster, or tire salesperson would be quick to dub it an "act of terrorism."

And yet on some intuitive level, we want to call the Manila happening a "nuisance crime." That is largely because no one was injured and, annoying as it is to have a flat tire, there is no universally recognized human right to such inflation.

This illustrates how complicated it is to define terrorism. Indeed, over the past few years, scholars and pundits have debated the question endlessly. One survey discovered 109 different definitions.[237] Some human rights groups have been particularly exercised about

the fact that there is no single universally agreed upon legal description of the phenomenon. Because of that lacuna and the concern
that the label will be used for political rather than purely descriptive
purposes, the official policy of my own organization, Amnesty
International, as determined by our international headquarters, is to
use the word "terrorism" only in quotes and to use the phrase
"armed opposition groups" to refer to terrorist operatives.[238]

Much as I regret to say it, I think that is unfortunate. Because
while there are different types of terrorism, just as there are different types of murder, the basic elements are the same: *non-state
actors (to use the technical term) committing acts of violence against
"noncombatant targets," involving violations of those targets' human
rights, for some larger political or religious purpose.* I certainly
appreciate the need for the international community to come to
consensus on a definition, but for human rights groups in particular
to be hesitant to call "terrorism" terrorism reinforces the suspicion
that we care more for the purity of our thought than the protection
of human lives. My favorite sin in the panoply of sins recognized by
the Roman Catholic church is the sin of "overscrupulosity" and in
this respect we human rights advocates are being overscrupulous.

Our sinning has, however, been the result of flawed thinking
rather than bad intent and hence has been of a venial rather than a
mortal nature. On the one hand, we have been guilty of giving cre-
dence to the oft-repeated observation that "one person's 'terrorist' is
another person's 'freedom fighter.'" On the other, we have been side-
tracked by the notion that governments, too, are guilty of inflicting
terrible violence on innocent populations and hence responsible for
"state terrorism." In the first instance we have worried that the label
would be applied too broadly; in the second, not broadly enough.

There is no question of course that the word "terrorist" has been
bandied about throughout history to denote practically anyone of
whom the prevailing powers disapproved. In Pharaoh's eyes, Moses

and Aaron no doubt deserved the label with their uncanny ability to utilize frogs and gnats and locusts in the interests of their people's liberation. John Brown is considered a hero today, but he would have been called a terrorist in 1856 when he led the Pottawatomie Massacre that resulted in the deaths of five Kansas slave owners. The British certainly regarded Menachem Begin as a terrorist when he fought with the Irgun in 1943 for a Jewish state in Palestine, though they and the rest of the world hailed him in 1978 when he shared the Nobel Peace Prize with Anwar Sadat. Henry Kissinger famously encouraged the Argentine government during the "Dirty War" to get its terrorist problem under control as quickly as possible.[239] And there was no more feared terrorist by the apartheid government of South Africa than the man widely regarded today as the greatest living exemplar of moral courage, Nelson Mandela.

Nor has the usage of the term become less reckless in recent years. Hollywood would hardly be able to make an action picture today if terrorism were stricken from the subjects available to screenwriters. The vocabulary of Bush administration officials would be noticeably truncated if "terrorist" were excised from their lexicon. And political leaders of all stripes would have one less mighty epithet with which to insult their adversaries. The Vietnamese ambassador to the United Nations, for example, interrupted a speech at the U.N. Human Rights Commission last year to accuse the speaker of being a "terrorist." And who was the speaker? Mr. Kok Ksor, president of the Montagnard Foundation and disciple of Mahatma Gandhi's passive resistance, who was appealing to the commission to protect his people, the Montagnards of Vietnam's Central Highlands, from torture, sterilization, and religious persecution at the hands of the Vietnamese government—a cause they have pursued with determination but without the use of violence.[240]

But does the fact that the word has been overused, used inadvisably, or used for political or propaganda purposes warrant our discarding it altogether? If it did, we would have to start junk piling (or putting in quotation marks) all sorts of words that have been corrupted by politically inspired misapplication——words like "Holocaust" or "national security" or even "rights." (Protesting a ban on video poker parlors in South Carolina, one poker enthusiast insisted, "It's like the state telling me I have no rights. It's pretty close to being Communist."[241])

Yes, of course "one person's 'terrorist' is another person's 'freedom fighter,'" but some "freedom fighters" are terrorists and some are not. Gandhi was a "freedom fighter" who did not commit human rights violations. The Provisional IRA are "freedom fighters" who do. Even if the cause is just, the methods may still be considered terrorist. To the extent that the African National Congress (ANC) engaged in violent acts against civilians, justifiable as their struggle against apartheid was, they were engaging in terrorism. When nonstate actors target civilians and fundamental human rights are violated for some larger political or religious purpose, that is terrorism. Full stop.

Nor is the fact that the term *terrorism* is legally vague or lacking a universally agreed-upon definition a hindrance to our use of it.[242] Many legally reputable terms lack precise descriptions and must therefore be interpreted to be applied. The Convention Against Torture, as we have seen, prohibits "cruel, inhuman, and degrading treatment or punishment." The Geneva Conventions prohibit crimes against humanity and "other inhumane acts." Compared to those phrases, *terrorism* looks as precise as "a square is a figure with four equal sides." "Never argue with a fool in public," the old proverb has it, "because passersby may not know who's who." But when it comes to terrorists, we almost always do—if we apply the basic criteria evenhandedly.

This does not mean that respect for human rights requires one to be a pacifist. Violence is often employed in the name of human rights against repressive regimes and, while many people are, of course, committed to nonviolence on religious or philosophical grounds, that violence is not in and of itself a violation of human rights. Those whose human rights are being abused need not just "sit back and take it" nor is nonviolent civil disobedience their only option. In the face of unmitigated oppression, those struggling for freedom may resort to violence without subjecting themselves to censure on human rights grounds *if* they have exhausted all peaceful means of winning their liberty and *if* they target noncivilian combatants. Notice that I said above that "to the extent that the African National Congress (ANC) engaged in violent acts *against civilians*" during the struggle against apartheid, it was engaging in terrorism. To the extent that the South African police and military were the victims of ANC violence, I would not consider the actions necessarily acts of terror or violations of human rights, though they were indeed crimes under South African law.

The distinction I am making here may be a difficult one to grasp. I am not for a moment encouraging or defending attacks upon the police or military. I am only suggesting that the word "terrorism" be reserved for attacks upon civilians and not upon those wielders of force deployed by governments for the purpose of enforcing laws or engaging in combat. The killing of police is a crime; pretending to surrender under the cover of a white flag and then opening fire, as Iraqi soldiers reportedly did during the Iraq War, is a war crime. These acts can legitimately be prosecuted but they are not automatically acts of terror.[243]

Which leads us to the question about "state terrorism." Aren't police and military forces sometimes themselves the purveyors of terror? Ought not the pervasive nature of government repression around the world—the disappearance, torture, and execution of tens of thousands of civilians, often in the name of "fighting terrorism"—give us pause about adopting the name solely for the acts of nonstate actors? Aren't many states responsible for terror just as bad, just as "terrifying," as "sub national groups or clandestine agents" and often even worse?

Indeed, they are. And we have names for those acts—names like "police brutality," "torture in custody," "extrajudicial execution," "war crimes," "genocide." National governments have killed far more innocent people than terrorists ever have, hundreds of millions more. And states can certainly use or suborn tactics that we can properly label in an emotional sense "terroristic." But if we are to keep the use of the word "terrorism" within manageable boundaries, it makes sense to limit its application to groups separate from the state (except of course where a state is so closely identified with terrorists or acquiescent in terrorism, as Libya was in the Lockerbie bombing, that it is impossible to tell the state and the terrorists apart, in which case we can properly speak of "state-sponsored terrorism"). This does not vitiate the horror of state crimes any more than the fact that the word *murder* is generally reserved for the acts of private citizens diminishes the horror of war crimes or state executions; it merely keeps the nomenclature cleaner.

Human rights advocates should have no hesitation using the word *terrorism* and roundly condemning it. It is anathema to everything for which we stand. We are unalterably opposed to all those who would employ the violation of other people's rights as a means to accomplish their own ends, and we should say so without equivocation. Our job is to help stop things like the attacks of 9/11 from happening and, inasmuch as we did not, we were among the many who failed. Human rights are designed to make the world a safer place. And though they wear the raiment of law (and hence must be attentive to legal distinctions), they are animated by concerns of the flesh. We who care about human rights are among the terrorists' most passionate adversaries.

• • •

To be effective foes of terrorism, then, requires of us two things: first, that we give up an absolutist understanding of rights and second, that we be willing to be prescriptive as well as reactive.

Some rights cannot be compromised under any circumstances. The International Covenant on Civil and Political Rights (ICCPR), to take one human rights treaty, is quite explicit on this point. The inherent right to life (Article 6), the right not to be subjected to torture or cruel, inhuman, and degrading treatment or punishment (Article 7), the right not to be enslaved (Article 8), the right to recognition as a person before the law (Article 16), the right to freedom of thought, conscience, and religion (article 18), and several others—these can never be derogated.[244]

On the other hand, "in time of public emergency which threatens the life of the nation," states parties to the ICCPR "may take measures derogating from their obligations" with regard to other provisions of the covenant, such as the right to liberty of movement (Article 12) and the rights surrounding criminal prosecution (Article 14). Compromises of these rights must only be "to the extent strictly required by the exigencies of the situation"; they must not be "inconsistent with . . . other obligations under international law"; they must "not involve discrimination solely on the ground of race, colour, sex, language, religion, or social origin"; and the government availing itself of the right of derogation must inform all other States Parties to the covenant of which rights are being compromised and why. Nonetheless, even the ICCPR recognizes that *in extremis* not all rights must be enforced absolutely. What constitutes *extremis*, a "public emergency which threatens the life of the nation"? Governments will generally set the bar too low, but human rights groups tend to be unwilling to admit that there is a bar at all. Determining where that bar is set, however, where the right balance lies between security and rights, is the major human rights challenge in an age of terror. It is foolish to think the problem is not complex.

Or to pretend that advances in democracy and respect for human rights, much as they are to be desired, carry no perils in and of themselves. When those Oberlin students of the late 1960s, to whom I alluded earlier, were not attending football games, they were engaging in political protests. The most dramatic took place one morning when about fifty students managed to stop and surround the car of a military recruiter as he drove into town intent upon lassoing young men and women into the armed forces that they might fight in Vietnam. The standoff lasted about three hours, the recruiter trapped in his car in the middle of the street, the students laughing and singing triumphantly around him. Every once in awhile the recruiter would try to inch his way forward to freedom, a tactic that was met with much angry shouting and the arrival of fresh student reinforcements. But finally the recruiter had had enough. "I'm sorry," he said. "I have to go to the bathroom." Someone handed him a cup. "No," he said, "I—I have to go to the bathroom. It's been three hours."

Now this development presented the students with a terrible dilemma. They were "radicals," after all, and the recruiter was the symbol of President Lyndon Johnson's hated War Machine, of napalm, deceit, murder. On the other hand, this one human being with his understandable human need was only indirectly the object of their ire; it was his job to do what he was doing, just as it was their job to stop him. And so, this being the era of "participatory democracy," the students took a vote. A majority decided that the recruiter should be freed to go relieve himself but *only* if he promised to return immediately to captivity. The recruiter promised. The sea of students outside his car door parted. The recruiter sprinted for the nearest john. The students awaited his return, the encircled car their prize, their trust unflagging in the honor of their sworn antagonist. Ten minutes went by. Twenty. Thirty. Until somebody shouted, "He's set up shop in Peters Hall. He's not taking a shit. He's not coming back. *He broke his promise.*" And at just that point a phalanx of police appeared, tear gas at the ready, to liberate the Federal government's property.

Democrats can be naive. Democracy is no panacea, particularly in the face of the unprincipled and brutish. It must often be introduced piecemeal, while simultaneously the infrastructure of the civil society that underlies democracy (a free press, nongovernmental organizations committed to nonviolent change, a corruption-free elections bureau, mores that require a peaceful transition of government, etc.) is built up gradually. Free elections are a *sine qua non* of democracy and respect for human rights, but they alone are not sufficient. Not sufficient to guarantee that human rights will be preserved. Not sufficient to ensure that peace and security will be maintained. Not sufficient to make certain that democracy itself will be there tomorrow. The United States is already learning this painful lesson in postwar Iraq, and if radical Islamists were brought to power in a democratic election, the United States might well rue the day it tried to bring "democracy" to that tragic land. More than one thug has assumed office through democratic vote. More than one lethal act has been perpetrated through the exercise of the freedoms of speech and association.[245] If, as a result of the exploitation of democracy and liberty, a state falls into the hands of terrorists or supplies terrorists with weapons of mass destruction, there will be no greater loser than the cause of human rights itself.

What better reason is there for we who care about human rights to be responsibly engaged in the struggle against terrorism than the fact that every time terrorism triumphs, not only are the rights of its victims dashed but the rights of the rest of us are put in danger of further erosion? When the Universal Declaration of Human Rights (UDHR) announces that "Everyone has the right to . . . security of person" (Article 3), it is engaging in no mere persiflage. It means what it says. And somehow this "security right" must be reconciled with all the other rights (what I have called "liberty rights") we are guaranteed, including the right to "a public trial" (Article 11), "freedom of movement . . . within the borders of each State " and (Article 13) the "right to peaceful assembly and association" (Article 20). Beyond the non-derogable rights, there is no room for absolutism.

So champions of human rights must be willing to provide prescriptions for the maintenance of public order as well as critiques of those charged with preserving it. The former is much more difficult than the latter. But the UDHR allows that limitations on rights and freedoms may be imposed "for the purpose of securing due recognition and respect for the rights and freedoms of others and of meeting the just requirements of morality, public order and the general welfare in a democratic society" (Article 29). Part of the human rights task, and a greatly neglected part, is to describe those circumstances.

The ICCPR provides us a series of hints. Certain rights may be limited "to the extent strictly required by the exigencies of the situation." This means at the very least that the circumstances must be dire, the limitations a last resort, and the violation as minimal as possible. One can infer that those limitations must also be effective. It goes without saying that individuals will interpret these criteria differently. But at a minimum they provide us a start at sketching out a theory of appropriate limits to rights.

• • •

The situation must be dire. Four people died in the anthrax scare of fall 2001. Their deaths were tragic but they alone were not enough to warrant suspension of rights. On the other hand, if massive quantities of anthrax had been distributed through the mails and thousands fallen victim, the circumstances might well be labeled dire, even catastrophic. It is irresponsible not to consider worst-case scenarios: induced meltdowns of nuclear reactors; the explosion of nuclear devices; mass contamination of big city water supplies; the spread of biological toxins; tens of thousands dead and dying.

None of these fearful developments can be predicted for certain but none of them are inconceivable either. In order to justify the suspension of rights, there must be strong evidence to believe that the danger is real, if not imminent. After all, the ICCPR allows the derogation of rights only in the case of "a public emergency that threatens the life of the nation." We know from bitter experience that repressive governments have been all too eager to proclaim "public emergencies" that threaten "the life of the nation" when all those "emergencies" really threatened was the life of the regime.

To "threaten *the life*" of a nation as large and powerful as the United States requires an incident of shattering proportions. Such developments do not come along every day but neither can we pretend any longer that they might never make an appearance. Did the events of September 11 qualify? Here is one legal scholar's description of an emergency sufficient to "threaten the life of the nation:"

> [It] must imperil some fundamental element of statehood or survival of the population—for example, the functioning of a major constitutional organ, such as the judiciary or legislative, or the flow of vital supplies. . . . A risk of detachment or loss of control over an important region [of a country] would appear to be sufficient. . . . Derogation would not be permissible in the case of a war that did not threaten the . . . "independence or security" of the . . . state. For example, involvement in foreign hostilities that did not threaten attack or have a significant impact on domestic institutions . . . would not meet the threshold.[246]

Under this definition, while the incidents on 9/11 may not have threatened the very existence of the nation, a case can surely be made that the larger nexus of developments of which they were a part have threatened the security of the state. Some derogation would therefore appear to have been warranted, at least in the weeks following the attack. Whether they still are is something about which the government is under obligation not just to orate but to demonstrate.

Curtailment of rights must be a last resort. The consequences of suspending or rolling back established rights are profound. None of those rights were created on a whim. If there are other ways to protect "the life of the state," they must be tried first before any rights are sacrificed. The state should be able to show that derogation was an absolute necessity.

The decision by the government to label American citizens Jose Padilla and Yaser Hamdi "unlawful combatants," not charge them with a crime but detain them indefinitely and deny them access to attorneys, thereby preventing them from proving their innocence and winning their release provides a case worth examining under what might be called the "necessity test." Federal officials claim that offering counsel to these two might compromise the interrogations they are undergoing, presumably because attorneys might advise them to stop talking.[247] But plea bargaining, in which information is traded for a lesser sentence, is common in the American judicial system. Trials at which the cumulative evidence convinces the accused to cooperate with prosecutors occur every day. Conviction often brings with it greater flexibility on the defendant's part before final sentence is pronounced. Imprisonment sometimes motivates prisoners to talk. If as basic a right as the right to counsel is to be breached, the government is under clear obligation to demonstrate that none of these techniques, which have worked so well in cases ranging from Mafia hit men to other terrorist suspects, would work in the Padilla and Hamdi cases.[248] Similarly, the government must show that there is no reasonable way to overcome its refusal to allow Zacarias Moussaoui to defend himself adequately against a capital charge by deposing Ramzi bin al-Shibh, the planner of 9/11 who Moussaoui claims could prove him innocent. Surely if a man is to be put to death, curtailment of his right to mount a defense can only be justi-fied (if it could be justified at all) if all means had been exhausted to both allow the deposition and protect the nation's security.

Or consider provisions of the Patriot Act that allow the government to demand that libraries turn over information about who has bor-rowed what books. No one would dispute that law enforcement offi-cers are perfectly justified in going to court, demonstrating the need for a warrant and obtaining a subpoena for the library records of an individual they have reason to suspect may be involved in a crime. But to give the FBI carte blanche to review anyone's library record (or their medical records or their Internet usage) simply by certifying to a judge (who cannot reject the application) that such a search is part of an ongoing terrorism investigation, absent evidence that such power has been demonstrated to be necessary to stop terrorism, is to impinge upon Article 19 of the UDHR ("Everyone has the right to . . . seek, receive, and impart information and ideas through any media. . . . ") without adequate justification. On what basis have other approaches to the problem (such as the traditional subpoena route) been shown to be inadequate? We know that the government could have reviewed every library and medical record in the country, and it would not have stopped the September 11 hijackers.

The limitations must be as minimal as possible to meet the necessity. The cliché "Give them an inch and they take a mile" could well have been invented to refer to public officials. Governments are notorious for overstepping appropriate bound-aries in the exercise of their power. Indeed, as we have seen, that is one reason we have the concept of rights in the first place. When the ICCPR says compromises of rights must be "to the extent strictly required" by the situation, it means that those compromises must be as restricted as possible consistent with the accomplishment of the goal. They must, in other words, be *proportional* to the end in sight.

The United States had every right to detain foreign nationals whom it suspected of involvement with 9/11 in the weeks following the attacks. It had every right to deport those who were in violation of their visas. What it did not have the right to do was to prevent those individuals from having timely access to their families and to counsel, timely information about what they were suspected of and timely disposition of their cases. (If it can be shown that racial or religious discrimination was the sole criterion behind the selection of detainees, that too is disallowed.) The rounding up of some foreign nationals, this is to say, might arguably meet the necessity test, but their subsequent treatment appears to have failed the "proportionality test."

The practices must be effective. Which leads to a fourth criterion by which to judge proposals to limit rights: namely, the likelihood that they will accomplish their proposed ends. After all, if we are going to monkey with human rights, we had best have the strongest possible reason to believe that such adjustments are actually practical and will truly make us safer.

The New York City police briefly took up the practice of questioning everyone arrested at antiwar rallies about their prior political activity and then recording the information in a database. After an outcry, the police abandoned the practice, not only because civil libertarians had objected but also, according to a department spokesperson, because it was "not critical to our needs" (in other words, it wasn't an effective use of time and resources.)[249] In early 2002, the Justice Department singled out for voluntary interviews about 5,000 Middle Eastern men living in the United States on immigrant visas. A senior law enforcement official subsequently described those interviews as "totally worthless," which ought to give the government pause with regard to its current policy of requiring all foreign nationals from twenty countries resident in the

United States to register.[250] Or, to take the library example again, what reason is there to think that the F.B.I. could ever have the resources to monitor every potentially suspicious library transaction or that this would be the best use of those resources even if they did? Furthermore, if the authorities did succeed in tracking those who had checked out a certain book, other authors, aware that language is endlessly elastic, would come along to make the same or similar points in more evasive, metaphorical, or indirect ways.

Romania under the savage dictatorship of Nicolae Ceausescu required that every typewriter in the country be registered with the government in order that if a typed statement critical of the regime was discovered, it could be traced to a particular typewriter and, presumably, its owner. The only problem was that the government was soon drowning in typewriter registrations and lacked the requisite experts to match type to suspicious document, anyway. And of course, despite the police state he maintained, when the end came, Ceausescu fell from power and was executed within a matter of days. His violations of his people's human rights were not only capricious; they were ultimately useless.

Add to these four criteria four more from the ICCPR—**limitations on rights must not compromise other obligations the state has under international law; they must not involve discrimination solely on the basis of race, color, sex, language, religion, or social origin; they must be temporary** (i. e., only while the public emergency lasts, which means that if we are going to suspend or modify certain rights, you must continue to ask at regular intervals, "Is the threat still imminent? Is the suspension still necessary?")[251]; and **they are subject to international scrutiny** because they must be reported and accounted for to the other states parties to the covenant—and we have a basis upon which to judge the proper balance between the right to security of person and other rights we want to claim.

Using these measures, we might conclude, for example, that video cameras in the New York City subway system are an acceptable compromise with our privacy. (The subway is vulnerable to real threats; given the limited number of police to patrol the subways, cameras meet the necessity test—they are less intrusive than personal searches or forcing subway riders to apply for licenses, thus satisfying the proportionality test. Cameras monitored by guards may be the most effective way to protect patrons; and such surveillance is in no way discriminatory, etc.) Whereas the Total Information Awareness Program that was proposed by the Defense Department and would provide government officials with immediate access to a host of personal data, such as phone calls, financial statements, and medical records on every U.S. resident was not. Similarly, a mandatory—or, alternatively, optional—national identification card for both citizens and noncitizens that could be used for a limited set of purposes, such as gaining entry to government buildings or boarding airplanes, while it could surely be abused, might well be a less onerous compromise of previously established rights than, say, the F.B.I.'s decision to count (and thereby potentially identify for special attention) all Muslims and mosques in the United States.[252]

But whatever our conclusions about specific proposals, my larger point is this: to be in favor of respect for human rights is not simply to be opposed to their abuse. That is the easy part. It is also to carry the responsibility of envisioning a world free of *all* human rights violations, whether committed by the state or committed by terrorists. It is therefore up to us to try to describe what such a world would look like and how we might get there. After all, if a *government* had been responsible for killing close to 3,000 civilians in one day, as the 9/11 terrorists were, human rights organizations would have spared no effort to expose the abuse and devise plans to counter its reoccurrence. But no such effort has, to my knowledge, ever been undertaken by an international human rights organization to counter Al Qaeda.

It is more than ironic that if, as I have argued earlier, human rights are not derived from natural law but from consensus of the international community, then they are far more adaptable to new circumstances than they would be if they somehow adhered in human beings "naturally." In the latter case, to compromise a natural right would be to sacrifice something utterly fundamental about being human. Conservative advocates of natural law theory apparently fail to see that it is only the more flexible approach of consensualism that offers the possibility of reconciling new understandings of human rights to a new and changing world.

What ought to be obvious to everyone is that we will not get to such a world by walking in a straight line. Life is more complicated than that, and we who care about human rights ought to admit it. Nor will we will get there by a few of us maintaining our moral purity while many of the rest of us lose our lives. We will only get there through a wise balance of "liberty rights" and "security rights," through an effective combination of security measures, economic equity, and increasing recognition of the contribution liberty makes to keeping us safe. Security and liberty are not either-or propositions; they constitute no zero-sum game. Getting that combination right is an immensely complicated calculus. Too complicated to leave to the generals, police chiefs, and politicians. As human rights advocates, we must stop thinking of those types of people merely as adversaries and start thinking of them as potential partners. For in a world scarred by terror, the truth is that we all really are in this together.

Human rights advocates tend to care largely for getting the rules right and sticking to them, whatever the consequences. This is a legacy of John Stuart Mill and laissez-faire liberalism. But at some point we need to step back and ask ourselves whether the rules we are following will truly get us where we want to go, whether the ultimate *outcome* of rule-following will be more suffering or less. If the best bet is that it will be more, then we had better be prepared to modify the rules or explain why we won't. We who cherish human rights do not want to find ourselves defending an interpretation of the UDHR and other human rights treaties that parallels the theory of the U.S. Constitution known as "original intention," advocated by such figures as Robert Bork and Antonin Scalia. That is the notion that the intentions of those who first wrote the Constitution must guide its contemporary interpretation, regardless of how circumstances may have changed over the generations to make their original presuppositions outmoded. But that is exactly the danger we run if we fail to adapt those human rights instruments to the demands of a radically changed world.

This is not a question of abiding by rules or scrapping them; not a matter of virtuous means versus perfidious ends. It is a question of identifying what St. Augustine called our "overlapping loves," which presumably include *both* staying alive and being free, and then working in good faith as a community to realize them both. Haitian Gen. Henry Christophe had one simple rule for the soldiers under his command: "March forward until I tell you to stop." It is said that to impress visitors to his huge fortress, located on a mountaintop overlooking the crashing ocean, he would parade his troops on the battlements of the fortress from which whole squadrons, not having received the order to stop, would plunge to their deaths in the sea. Now is the time to ask ourselves whether our rules are flexible enough to avoid such a fate.

CHAPTER 9 Sitting on Our Bayonets

The Role of Human Rights in the Struggle against Terrorism

At some point we may be the only ones left. That's OK with me. We are America.[253]

George W. Bush

When I was growing up in Pittsburgh in the early 1960s, I was afraid of just two things. I was afraid of nuclear war and I was afraid of Tony Santaguido.

I was afraid of nuclear war because my parents had assured me that, should war come, Pittsburgh's steel mills would be among the first targets the Russians bombed. When I learned in school, however, that if I were simply to "duck and cover" under my wooden desk, I would be safe from radiation, I immediately relegated nuclear war to a much less prominent place in my litany of worries.

But that left Tony Santaguido, the neighborhood bully. Tony didn't actually live in our immediate neighborhood—he lived several blocks away—but he and his gang would show up without warning every few weeks and wreak their havoc on us "good kids."

One time Tony caught me with a left hook to the jaw that persuaded me on the spot to go into the ministry.

The most obvious way to have dealt with Tony, I suppose, would have been to have bloodied his nose right back, and, if I had been one to do my fighting with anything other than words, I probably would have taken that approach. But I was not confident of my skills as a pugilist, and I knew that Tony had a large family. I suspected that if I did by some miracle manage to prevail, his brothers or cousins would have sought me out to exact their revenge, and I would have been living in a world of perpetual fear that might have made the alternative of nuclear war seem welcome.

So I settled on a different tack. I made sure in the first place to surround myself with as large a group of my friends as possible whenever I scented that Tony might be on the prowl, and I decided to try to strike up an acquaintance with one or two of Tony's own gang who weren't as ill-disposed toward me as he was. I wanted to find out what he had against me, convince them I wasn't such a bad guy after all, and have them prevail upon him to leave me alone.

After a time and somewhat to my surprise, these dual tactics began to work. Tony still glared at me when we crossed paths but, as long as I had allies with me, he left me alone. The real test, however, came one afternoon when he and three or four of his cohorts chanced upon me as I walked alone home from school. "There's that little shit!" Tony said, which wasn't quite an accurate description because the fact was that I was scared shitless. I looked pleadingly at my contacts among his gang. One of them shrugged. "The fucker ain't worth our time," he said. "C'mon." Tony hesitated, but then, like all bullies, realized that if his gang wasn't with him, it might not be wise to pursue the fight. "Fucker," he said, and moved on. I never knew what exactly had changed the dynamics within Tony's gang, but I figure now that it had something to do with Casey Stengel's famous observation that "the secret of a great [baseball] manager is to keep the two guys who hate your guts away from the three guys who are undecided."

I also figure that this little parable has a thing or two to teach us about fighting terrorism. On the face of it, the best course would have been for me to have beaten Tony senseless and, indeed, if my friends and I had had the wherewithal to do that, we would have pursued that option and that would have put an end to our immediate problems. Sometimes you just have to stand up to bullies. But, as Talleyrand observed, you can do anything with a bayonet except sit on it, and, if we had taken the martial course and stopped there, not bothering to nurture our own alliance with one another or find ways to reach out to the more persuadable segments of Tony's retinue, the three guys who were undecided, we might well have been in for a long, nasty battle with either a resurgent Tony or his proxies.

The wisest thing to do would have been to have cleverly combined measured strength with allied solidarity and an overture or two to the most receptive elements of our adversaries. That way we would have created a neighborhood built on appropriate doses of both hard power and soft, force and diplomacy, order and law. The United States government has gotten the bayonet work down perfectly in the war on terror, but it keeps trying to sit on the tip. Contrarily, some observers would have us believe that if we merely sit long enough on the comfortable cushions of soft power, diplomacy, and respect for international law, we will usher in a world in which bayonets are hardly necessary. Both approaches risk serious injury and neither by itself will put an end to terrorism. Finding the right balance will not only make for a more secure world; it will rescue the credibility of human rights from the proverbial slough of despond.

• • •

When those 3,000 people died on September 11, 2001 the meaning of their individual lives was immediately transposed in the minds of hundreds of millions of people around the world into something larger, a symbol of the best of the American tradition, a proud legacy of liberty, generosity, freedom, and respect for human rights. A headline in a French newspaper caught the spirit perfectly: "Nous sommes tous Americains," it read: "We are all Americans."

Those who died that day, regardless of the realities of their respective lives, stood in for all people around the globe who wish little more than to live productively, care for their children, do no harm to their neighbors, spread good will as it is given to them, and stave off the magnet of death. So moving was their fate that the living reached deep inside themselves to do them honor. One example will suffice. A ministerial colleague of mine whose ex-wife died on the 97th floor of Tower One wished to plant a cherry tree in her honor outside her home in Brooklyn. My colleague and the couple's daughter approached the owner, age seventy, of a local nursery in Plymouth, Massachusetts, where they lived, but were told that no cherry tree was in stock. "But I'll get you one," the owner said. The day of the planting ceremony arrived and my colleague went to the nursery to pick up the tree to drive it to New York City, but the owner was nowhere to be found. Finally, after much frantic calling, my colleague reached him on his cell phone. The owner was way down in southern New Jersey where he had finally located a cherry tree. He had called every nursery in New England and then driven in his old truck all the way down the Eastern seaboard in his search until he found what he was looking for. That afternoon he delivered it to Brooklyn and refused to be paid a penny.[254] September 11 brought out the best in us as a country and a people—the best that we can be.

Since then, however, that noble legacy has been tarnished. A year and a half after 9/11, the Pew Global Attitudes survey revealed that U.S. favorability ratings had dropped precipitously in almost every country polled—and this was several months *before* the divisive war in Iraq. Positive images of the United States in allied Muslim countries like Turkey and Pakistan had diminished 22 percent and 13 percent respectively over a previous survey done two years before. People in virtually every nation polled concluded that the United States acted unilaterally and failed to take the interests of their country into account in making international policy. Even in such friendly countries as Canada and Great Britain, majorities disliked the spread of American customs.[255]

No doubt it is inevitable that the world's richest and most powerful nation will generate a measure of resentment. Ours is a unipolar world and it is hardly realistic to expect the "hyperpower," as the French call the United States, to voluntarily sacrifice its interests or its might in pursuit of an abstract ideal of international comity. At the same time, for that hyperpower to fail to recognize the disadvantages of international opprobrium, to treat its friends dismissively, and its skeptics as adversaries, is to invite an ultimate catastrophe.

The United States' relations with the rest of the world turn on many things—on the use of our military, the health of our economy, the depth of our pockets, the resolution of the Israeli-Palestinian dispute, the tempering of our hubris, and the respect we pay those weaker than we. But they also depend to a degree that appears to have gone unrecognized by Washington of late, on the extent to which we honor human rights, respect the rule of international law, and model the kind of democratic civil society that we would encourage others to pursue. As Shakespeare put it in Act II of *Measure for Measure:* "O, it is excellent/To have a giant's strength; but it is tyrannous/To use it like a giant."

Similarly, victory in the war against terrorism depends upon a myriad of tactics—from tracking down terrorists to disrupting their finances to protecting cyberspace to building a coordinated system of homeland security. It requires a less oil-dependent economy in order that we might be less reticent to criticize oil-producing states. But it also depends upon nurturing relations with our allies who can supply intelligence and assist with law enforcement. It depends upon cultivating moderate factions within the Islamic community, both at home and abroad, who can counter the influence of radical Islamists. It depends upon addressing the complaints that feed the terrorist retinue—complaints about corruption, poverty, and lack of access to true democracy. It depends upon offering the world a better idea than the terrorists offer. And all these depend upon respect for human rights and the fragile scaffolding that undergirds them.

In the opening chapter, I outlined some of what we know about terrorists and Al Qaeda. I said that terrorists need to be out-thought and not just out-muscled. I said that terrorists depend upon a wide network of support, their retinue. I said that terrorists exploit poverty and alienation in the creation of that retinue. Of Al Qaeda I said that it played upon divisions within Islamic countries caused by dissatisfaction with corrupt, authoritarian rule; that it turned every misstep of the United States to its advantage by convincing Muslims that America was their enemy; and that it needed to be countered not just by force but by ideology and the encouragement of reform.

Here, then, are some of the ways human rights are crucial to winning the war on terrorism:

Respect for human rights diminishes the appeal of extremism. Human rights, as we have seen in chapter 5, are grounded in a broad international consensus as to what makes for a civilized world. They are adopted because they work—to minimize human suffering, to protect the weak, and to make societies more stable. By their very nature, human rights serve the cause of the more moderate elements in any culture. Those who would impose their views on others, who reject the autonomy of the individual, and who would undermine democracy and the norms that are required to make democracy work—all these will be enemies of human rights.

As the noted Jordanian journalist Rami Khouri put it, "It takes many years of political, economic, and human degradation to make a terrorist. So fighting terror can only succeed by rehumanizing degraded societies, by undoing, one by one, the many individual acts of repression, obstruction, denial, marginalization, and autocracy that cumulatively turned . . . decent, God-fearing people into animals that kill with terror."[256] Human rights are the handmaiden of that process. They are the scourge of corrupt regimes and the implacable foe of tyrants.

To the extent that the war on terror will be won by persuading the retinue to reject violence and seek change through democratic means, it will only be won with the help of human rights. To the extent that corruption in Muslim countries is routed and good government adopted, thereby depriving extremists of a keystone of their appeal, it will only be because the rights to dissent and to organize, to expose and to excoriate, have been embraced. To the extent that moderate Islam challenges its radical counterparts, it will do so, as it has in Iran, in tandem with openness to the kind of global values reflected in the struggle for human rights—support for the empowerment of women, for example, and rejection of the harsher interpretations of *shari'a*. To the extent that predominantly Muslim countries will recapture the glory of an enlightened Islamic past, swept up in learning and scientific advancement, they will do so only by adopting norms of tolerance, free inquiry, free movement, and free speech. And to the extent that repressive governments are inherently unstable governments providing breeding grounds for terrorism—Sudan, Uzbekistan, Kyrgystan—a human rights regimen offers the best hope of a peaceful transition to a liberal democratic state.

The United States is committed to promoting democracy around the globe. But democracy, as we have noted before, is a two-edged sword that can bring tyrants to power as easily as pluralists. If America is identified with autocratic regimes; if it is justifiably charged with ignoring inconvenient human rights claims; if it is seen as skirting the rules at home and undermining international human rights abroad, its promotion of democracy will be suspect and its insistence that others abide by the rule of law seen as a charade. As one Egyptian dissident put it with a rueful laugh, "John Ashcroft's arrests of Arab men, the treatment of prisoners at Guantanamo Bay, military tribunals—all of it is exported from here [Egypt]."[257] Nothing undermines the democracy agenda more thoroughly or extends a more welcome invitation to extremists than such hypocrisy. If we want to guarantee the victory of anti-American sentiment (in, for example, future elections in Iraq), we could do no better than to shortchange human rights.

Troubled though the struggle for democracy in Muslim countries has been, the notion that Islam is inherently incompatible with democracy and respect for human rights is belied by nascent movement toward greater democratic rule in places like Indonesia, Jordan, Morocco, Qatar, and Bahrain. Muslims in India, while a minority, have long been eager participants in that country's democratic politics. The secret is to seed and sustain moderation, to give democrats no reason to rue their choice of friends or of philosophy, and that will only come if their friends are models of rectitude and their philosophy the midwife of a truly civil state.

Respect for human rights, particularly economic, dries up the pool of terrorist recruits. Enamored of the "pioneer spirit" that inspired "rugged individualists" to "tame a continent," the United States has rarely been sympathetic to the notion of economic rights. Americans believe in equal *opportunity* for every individual but associate a *right* to "an adequate standard of living," "the highest attainable standard of . . . health," and "education . . . directed to the full development of the human personality," with collective economies long since discredited. That is one reason the United States has never ratified the International Covenant on Economic, Social, and Cultural Rights, from which these phrases come, despite the fact that there is nothing in that document that specifies how its rights are to be realized or repudiates a capitalist system. All this may account for the modest amount of international assistance the United States proffers. Total American spending on nonmilitary foreign aid in 2002 represented a mere 0.15 percent of gross domestic product, placing the United States last among twenty-one industrialized countries. On a more comprehensive measurement, the 2003 Commitment to Development Index prepared by the Center for Global Development and *Foreign Policy* magazine, gauging whether twenty-one countries' aid, trade, immigration, investment, peacekeeping, and environmental policies help or hurt poor countries, the United States finished next to last.[258]

Such penuriousness is hardly defensible under any circumstances. In a globalized economy in which the United States has become associated, fairly or not, with the excesses of an unregulated market and the absence of appropriate safety nets, it is downright dangerous, and that danger is multiplied when the United States appears to manipulate the market to its own advantage through protectionism. While no one believes that America can buy her way into the hearts of poor people, she certainly can make their lives considerably easier by championing economic justice in the form of debt relief, support for micro lending institutions, increased assistance to countries committed to good government and human rights, and generous follow-through in the rebuilding of Afghanistan and Iraq.

A more equitable distribution of the world's resources will not in and of itself put an end to terrorism, but it will reduce the appeal of those who would characterize the West as bloated and self-satisfied and demonstrate to the would-be retinue, the "undecided," that there may well be avenues more productive than the terroristic through which to meet their basic needs.

In his book *Why Terrorism Works*, Alan Dershowitz argues that we should "never . . . try to understand or eliminate [terrorism's] alleged root causes," for that would "encourage the use of terrorism as a means toward achieving ends."[259] But Dershowitz is confusing root causes with proximate goals. For while it may well be wise to resist giving in to terrorists' demands, it is absurd not to try to reduce the conditions that encourage those susceptible to but not yet seduced by terrorism's siren song. As one Israeli defense official explained when asked, in the face of Ariel Sharon's crackdown on Palestinians, why all the arrests and killings had not brought an end to suicide attacks, "It's like we're mowing the grass. You mow the lawn one day and the next day the grass grows right back."[260] To resist terrorist blackmail is wise; to ignore the seeds that make such blackmail attractive is stupid. It is difficult, if not impossible, to deter the hard-core terrorist who has no fear of death, so the goal must be to reach those not yet converted to thanatophilia. President Bush has said that the war on terror will never end. He may or may not be correct, but one thing is for sure: we guarantee that conflict's perpetuity if we ignore what fuels it in the first place.

We knew this during the cold war—that struggling countries were more susceptible to the economics of collectivism than healthy ones—and we responded with favorable trade conditions, public works programs, and the Peace Corps. In similar vein, economically unstable states like Pakistan and eroding ones like Nepal (to say nothing of outright "failed" states like Somalia and Chechnya) are vulnerable to those who would exploit economic discontent for political gain. Like slaveholders in the pre-Civil War South who constantly feared that a few firebrands might ignite the smoldering resentments of large numbers of slaves, so Western economic powers ought rightly worry that extremists can easily spread their venom among the oppressed, thereby refurbishing their numbers. The solution in both cases: to set the economic captives free.

A few months after 9/11, Secretary of State Colin Powell visited Nepal, fraught as that country is by a Maoist insurgency. A Nepalese reporter asked him whether or not the roots of Maoist violence might be successfully addressed through "some wonderful and good package programs towards alleviation of poverty and the creating plenty of job opportunities." The secretary replied in one word: "Yes."[261]

Respect for human rights puts the lie to the claim that the war on terror is a war on Islam. One of the least successful elements of the Bush administration's war on terror was a series of advertisements featuring Muslim Americans extolling the virtues of the American way of life. Modeled on the public information efforts of Radio Free Europe during the cold war and designed to be placed on Al Jazeera and other media outlets serving the Arab world, the campaign was wound down almost before it began. The problem was simple: during the days of Radio Free Europe, the United States was not singling out Eastern Europeans in America for special attention.

As long as the United States is perceived to be treating Muslims in a discriminatory fashion, requiring them and only them to register their presence as foreign nationals in the country, making it far more difficult for Muslim and only Muslim students (potentially some of America's strongest advocates) to get visas to study in the States, or deporting Muslims and only Muslims who have been productive residents and have sunk deep roots into American communities, the Islamic world will continue to understand the fight against terrorism as a fight against them. "Fearful, Angry or Confused, Muslim Immigrants Register," read a recent headline in the *New York Times*, a headline which we can be sure made its way, along with the feelings it described, across the seas.[262] As long as the United States fails to be evenhanded in its criticism of human rights abuses by Israelis and Palestinians or denies application of Geneva Conventions principles to the predominantly Muslim prisoners at Guantanamo Bay or aligns itself with repressive governments in

China, Russia, or Kazakhstan that are targeting Muslim minorities, it will be hard to convince the Muslim world—no matter how many Muslim lives the United States saved in Bosnia or how many mosques President Bush visits in Detroit—that anti-Muslim sentiment does not underlie the anti-terrorist campaign. And the more widespread that conviction, the easier for Al Qaeda it will be.

Respect for human rights restrains the unilateralist impulse. Some months ago a group of colleagues and I were engaged in a conversation with a high Bush administration official about the International Criminal Court (ICC). "Americans don't want a court that can supersede the American judicial system and conduct potentially unfair prosecutions of Americans," the official said. "Wait until the court has a success or two," I replied. "When Americans see torturers and tyrants being brought to justice in accordance with due process guarantees and without resort to violence—when, in other words, they see the rule of law actually *working* for the benefit of humankind, they may well think twice about how wise it is for the U.S. to resist the effort."

There are two problems with unilateralism, with regarding yourself as not bound by the rules that everybody else is. The first problem is that such exceptionalism alienates your friends, those countries upon which the United States must depend to fight the war on terror. How can we possibly track intercontinental movements of terrorists and their bankrolls without the cooperation of other countries? How can we gather intelligence, infiltrate foreign terrorist cells, collect evidence, and take suspects into custody without relying upon the good will of foreign intelligence and law enforcement bodies? If any enterprise is inherently multilateral in its nature, stopping terrorism is. But so is respecting human rights for the very foundation of human rights is a commitment to universal values and global enforcement mechanisms. If the United States is seen as undermining those values and those institutions, be it by hamstringing the ICC, ignoring the Geneva Conventions, discrediting the U.N. or flaunting its use of the death penalty, many of those allies will fade away or at least be far more reluctant partners on the case.

And the second problem with unilateralism is that it encourages your adversaries to act likewise. If the United States can thumb its nose at international law, why shouldn't everybody else? No matter how powerful the U.S. military, it can never patrol every corner of the globe at once. Surely it is better to persuade as many nations as possible to adopt common standards of self-enforcing behavior consistent with respect for law and human rights. Al Qaeda is found in at least eighty countries. Surely it is to our long-term advantage to encourage as many of those countries as possible to restrain their own impulses toward unilateralism, toward finding a homegrown "terrorist" under every opposition party rock, and join in a collective, worldwide campaign to stop the real terrorism that threatens all of us. We can hardly expect to do that successfully if we ourselves fail to trim our sails to the global wind.

The United States possesses enormous, unparalleled power. When we act multilaterally, we make that power more acceptable to others. We engender less resentment, we stimulate less envy. And we create norms and structures that will serve us well when that day comes, as it inevitably will, when our power is no longer unparalleled after all.

Respect for human rights offers the world a transforming vision. I am often proud of the international human rights movement but never more so than when it plays the role of the "equal opportunity offender." On these occasions Amnesty International and other human rights defenders are called upon to set aside personal political predilection, doctrine, or ideology and "call them as we see them." Some of us may not sympathize, for example, with American policy toward Cuba, but when Fidel Castro imprisons dozens of peaceful dissidents and executes three people for hijacking a ferry in order to reach freedom, we must call the wrath of heaven down on his repression. Regardless of our individual perspectives on the Israeli-Palestinian conflict, both sides have committed serious human rights violations, and someone must assume the job of calling them to account, no matter what the consequences. The same is true in Kashmir, Colombia, the Democratic Republic of Congo (DRC), or wherever parties would strip humans of their dignity in pursuit of a "precious cause."

What provides the authority for us to make these judgments, imperfect though our sight may be, is the presence of a common plumb line and a universal language. Human rights values transcend culture, ideology, and faith in service to that which is recognizable to all: the human face of suffering. Differ though they may on the details, Muslim, Christian, Buddhist, Jew, Swedish socialist or Zurich banker, Texas pol or Turkish elder, all agree that the innocent deserve protection, the accused deserve defense, the weak ought not be trampled, and torture cannot stand. David Rifkin, a Washington attorney, referring to those accused of being Saddam Hussein's henchmen, said, "Try them for a week. Give them a chance to say what they have to say and then execute the senior ones. Is there any doubt they're guilty?"[263] Thanks to the growth of a human rights culture, thinking people all over the world can see why that's a travesty.

Some have suggested that human rights provide the universal faith that no one religion can aspire to. But human rights fail as a religious faith: unlike religion, their goal is to stave off death altogether, not teach us reconciliation to it. Human rights do no more than point to a higher mode of civilization, call us to a better polity, invoke a more just economy, but, even were we to achieve all that, we would still be left with those vagaries of the human heart—the impulse to do evil, for example—that no exercise of rights can vitiate. Religion this is not. And yet, is not that vision of a more civilized society itself an exaltation? The world is desperate for even a modest platform that its people can agree on. Human rights come closer than anything else yet thought of and those nations that would be their champion, so they will be the human race's inspiration.

• • •

A week or so before the 2003 war in Iraq rushed to its conclusion, I was speaking at the University of Kansas in Lawrence. Most of the audience in this oasis of liberal thought were opposed to what the United States was doing, but one man put to me an utterly appropriate question: "How do you reconcile your abhorrence of Saddam Hussein's human rights record with opposition to the war? Wouldn't you like to see similar thugs removed from power all over the world?" "You bet I would," I said, "but I speak now not for Amnesty International but for myself. I am not inherently opposed to military intervention, certainly not in the service of human rights if the odds are good that such intervention will stop more suffering than it will cause. My problem in this case is that the United States undertook a 'preventive war' in violation of the United Nations Charter under the cover of human rights without first doing everything it could to convince key allies, much less the world, that there was something that needed preventing in the first place. The United States played the roughneck who doesn't give a damn what others think. But those key allies—France, Germany, Russia—also were at fault for they played the role of the aesthete, more concerned for their piety, for keeping their reputations clean and hands unsullied, than for ending pain or derailing future suffering. The good news is that Saddam Hussein will soon be gone. The bad news is that all the players in the drama conspired to make the world less stable in the process."

After the program was over, a young man approached me with a troubled look. "Do you mean to say," he began, "that if the Security Council had approved intervention in Iraq, you personally would have had no problem with it, even if you knew that 5,000 people would die?" "It is not an easy question," I replied. "But if I knew that far more than 5,000 people would be saved and I thought there was no other way to save them, how could I possibly not consider it?"

These are the kind of real-life quandaries policy makers face every day. Unlike torture, authorized international force is not *ipso facto* beyond the pale. Unlike the hypothetical case of a ticking bomb in which it is impossible to know what the ultimate utilitarian calculus will be, the numbers who are suffering—*right now, today*—in Liberia, Chechnya, China, or the DRC are well known and very real. Just because George W. Bush, like virtually all presidents before him, uses human rights like a bad cook uses a spice—to cover up the taste of otherwise unpalatable policies—doesn't mean that human rights do not sometimes require a big stick in addition to soft speaking. The Europeans, for all their righteousness about human rights, did virtually nothing to stop the slaughter in Bosnia. Human rights are not for the faint of heart; they are not the province of wimps, but of the stubborn and the robust.

That the United States has been giving the struggle against terrorism a bad name of late does not mean that the fears that motivate that struggle are not legitimate and clear. I have described the many ways in which the United States government has tainted the legacy of those who died on 9/11 by sacrificing fundamental principles that have long characterized the best that America could be. But it taints that legacy just as surely for human rights advocates to play the aesthete, to duck the questions, for example, about how we control weapons of mass destruction (WMD)—the use of which would constitute a human rights crime of enormous proportions—without intercepting them preventively. To adapt international law to new realities is in no way to excuse American unilateralism. Quite the contrary. It is to insist that that we all face a new world and it is up to all of us to try to solve it. To insist that global threats be met by global responsibility is at the heart of the human rights ethos.

In contrast, consider one of the most widely read books in 2002, Robert Kaplan's *Warrior Politics: Why Leadership Demands a Pagan Ethos*. Kaplan has made a career out of playing the Cassandra when it comes to worldwide poverty, disease, disruption, and instability. His tragic view of life, it was said, convinced Bill Clinton, who had read Kaplan's *Balkan Ghosts*, to defer intervening in Bosnia for fear the conflict was intractable. But in *Warrior Politics,* Kaplan thinks he has the answer. "The more hopeless history and geography appear to be . . . ," he says, "the more prolific the opportunities for heroism." And who will play the hero? "'Historically,'" Kaplan quotes the political philosopher E. H. Carr, "'every approach in the past to a world society has been the product of the ascendancy of a single Power.'" The United States "and nobody else will write the terms for international society," Kaplan concludes and puts that sentence in *italics*. As to human rights, they "are ultimately and most assuredly promoted by the preservation and augmentation of American power."[264]

If Kaplan is right, it is more important than ever that the United States model respect for human rights for, under his scenario, America and America alone will be setting the norms and standards by which the rest of the world lives. (Had Kaplan influenced still another president?) But look at Carr's words closely: "every *approach* in the past to world society has been the product of the ascendancy of a single Power." Every one of those unilateral "approaches" has failed and every one of those single Powers has eventually faded away. Might it not be time, in the face of the common enemy of terrorism, to try another way? Might it not be time to recognize that, while the United States has and will for the foreseeable future continue to have an enormous impact on "the terms for international society," those terms will only last, those rules will only be obeyed, if they have emerged from multiple sources, meet the needs of many players, and can claim the enthusiasm of the world community.

If human rights depend upon American power, it is more important than ever that this power be used with grace and care. Otherwise that city set on a hill shall find that it has "open[ed] the mouths of enemies to speak evil of the ways of God" and America "shall surely perish out of the good land whither we pass over this vast sea. . . . " The truth is that, however dependent human rights may be upon the "preservation and augmentation of American power," American power is just as dependent for its preservation upon its fidelity to human rights. True though E. H. Carr's historical maxim may be, it is just as true that power not grounded in justice and not *recognized* as just by those subjected to it eventually does not stand. Human rights provide leaven to power.

• • •

Uncle Shumi escaped the Nazis but just barely and, when he returned to his hometown for a visit after the war, a group of gentile children taunted him: "The dead Jews have come back," they shouted. But Shumi just stood his ground. Stood his ground and returned to the village regularly, reaching out to the children and telling them stories. Eventually the whole village looked forward to his visits and, when he died, the six children who had taunted him said Kaddish at his grave.[265]

Human rights emerge out of the common misery of humankind and give voice to the simplest needs of the human spirit. They teach that bodies all perish but that evil does too. They help us to recognize evil and combat it but to be temperate in triumph. "Conduct your triumph," said Lao-tzu, "as a funeral." Guard well that which you cherish but remember that a generous heart is what makes what you cherish worth guarding.

END NOTES

1. "A Nation Challenged: the Detainees," *New York Times*, December 5, 2001.

2. Article 9(2) of the International Covenant on Civil and Political Rights, ratified by the United States in 1992, provides that "Anyone who is arrested shall be informed at the time of arrest of the reasons for his arrest and shall promptly be informed of any charges against him."

3. Goldberg was in fact paraphrasing Justice Robert Jackson's dissenting opinion in *Terminiello* v. *Chicago* (1949) in which Jackson wrote, "It is between liberty with order and anarchy without. There is danger that, if the Court does not temper its doctrinaire logic with a little practical wisdom, it will convert the Constitutional Bill of Rights into a suicide pact."

4. Another example might be the need to restrict the "freedom of peaceful assembly" (Article 20) in the face of an epidemic involving a highly contagious disease.

5. In his December 6, 2001 testimony before the Senate Judiciary Committee defending Justice Department actions in the months following 9/11, Attorney General John Ashcroft said, "We are at war with an enemy who abuses individual rights as it abuses jet airliners: as weapons with which to kill Americans," clearly implying that such rights might need to be curtailed. A few weeks earlier Supreme Court Justice Sandra Day O'Connor had told a group of New York University law students, without lamentation, "We're likely to experience more restrictions on personal freedom than has ever been the case in our country." (vanden Heuvel, Katrina, ed., *A Just Response:* The Nation *on Terrorism, Democracy, and September 11, 2001*, New York: Nation Books, 2002, p. 59.)

6. Michael Ratner of the Center for Constitutional Rights, for one, has said that "the idea that by curtailing civil liberties . . . we will somehow create a fortress America that will make us safe from terrorism is absurd." ("Building Post-9/11 Security: Permanent War Abroad and Permanent War at Home," www.humanrightsnow.org).

7. The poll conducted by National Public Radio, the Kaiser Family Foundation, and Harvard's Kennedy School of Government was described in "Poll: Security Trumps Civil Liberties," at www.npr.org, November 30, 2001.

8. "How Far Americans Would Go to Fight Terror," *Christian Science Monitor*, November 14, 2001, describing a *Monitor*/TIPP poll. Other polls have reported as many as 45 percent of Americans agreeing that torture was acceptable.

9. *Op. Cit.*, "Poll: Security Trumps Civil Liberties."

10. "Feeling Secure, U.S. Failed to See, or Stop, a Determined Enemy," *New York Times*, September 8, 2002.

11. Ignatieff, Michael, "Is the Human Rights Era Ending?" *New York Times*, February 5, 2002.

12. Adapted from Mao Tse-tung's aphorism "Guerillas are the fish and the people are the sea."

13. "How Two Lives Met in Death," *Newsweek*, April 15, 2002.

14. Wright, Lawrence, "The Man Behind bin Laden," *New Yorker*, September 16, 2002.

15. Bush, George W., "Securing Freedom's Triumph," *New York Times*, September 11, 2002.

16. Klusmeyer, Douglas, and Astri Suhrke, "Comprehending 'Evil': Challenges for Law Policy," *Ethics & International Affairs,* vol. 16, No. 1, 2002, provides an excellent discussion of these issues.

17. Hudson, Rex A., "The Sociology and Psychology of Terrorism: Who Becomes a Terrorist and Why?" Library of Congress, September 1999, p. 25. Some F.B.I. and C.I.A. officials have speculated that the so-called twentieth hijacker, Zacarias Moussaoui, was not included in the final 9/11 operations because he was simply "far too volatile and unstable to handle a long-term undercover operation." (Hersh, Seymour M., "The Twentieth Man," *New Yorker*, September 30, 2002, p. 56.)

18. See Ohnuki-Tierney, *Emiko Kamikaze, Cherry Blossoms, and Nationalists: The Militarization of Aesthetics in Japanese History*, Chicago: University of Chicago Press, 2002.

19. Levy, Marion J., Jr., "Levy's Nine Laws of the Disillusionment of the True Liberal," *Midway,* Volume 10, winter, 1970. See Doran, Michael, "The Pragmatic Fanaticism of al Qaeda: An Anatomy of Extremism in Middle Eastern Politics," *Political Science Quarterly*, Summer, 2002.

20. *Ibid.*, p. 47. Says Ehud Sprinzak, dean of the Lauder School of Government, Policy, and Diplomacy at the Interdisciplinary Center in Herliya, Israel, "Organizations only implement suicide terrorism if their community . . . approves of its use." ("Rational Fanatics," *Foreign Policy*, September/October 2000, p. 72.) The Terrorism Research Center confirms the relationship between terrorism and popular support and cites examples: "Groups considering terrorism as an option ask a crucial question: Can terrorism induce enough anxiety to attain its goals without causing a backlash that will destroy the cause . . . ? In the early 1970s, the Tupamaros in Uruguay and the ERP (People's Revolutionary Army) and Montoneros in Argentina misjudged a hostile popular reaction to terrorism. They pushed their societies beyond their threshold of tolerance and were destroyed as a result." ("The Basics of Terrorism: Part 2, 'The Terrorists,' http://www.geocities.com/Capitol Hill/2468/bpart2.html).

21. Little, Allan, "Who is a Terrorist?" BBC News Global Policy Forum, December 6, 2001.

22. Pipes, Daniel, "God and Mammon: Does Poverty Cause Militant Islam?" *The National Interest*, Winter, 2001/02, p. 19. See also Pipes, Daniel, *Militant Islam Reaches America*, New York: W. W. Norton & Co., 2002, pp. 52–63.

23. See, for example, Russell, Charles A. and Bowman H. Miller, "Profile of a Terrorist," *Terrorism: An International Journal*, Vol. 1, No. 1, 1977, pp. 17–34, 1977.

24. "Terrorism: Q & A: Liberation Tigers of Tamil Eelam," Council on Foreign Relations website, June 28, 2002.

25. "A Boyhood on the Mean Streets of a Wealthy Emirate," *New York Times*, March 3, 2003.

26. *Op. Cit.*, Hersh, p. 72, referring to the work of University of Paris sociologist Farhad Khrorokhavar.

27. "Most members of the extremist Palestine Islamic Jihad," says Paul R. Pillar in *Terrorism and U.S. Foreign Policy* (Washington, DC: Brookings Institution Press, 2001, p. 31) "are of low social origin and live in poverty in the bleak neighborhoods or refugee camps of the Gaza Strip. Hamas also does its most successful recruiting in Gaza."

28. "Al-Qaeda Has a Small, Selective Core," *USA Today*, September 19, 2002.

29. Gunaratna, Rohan, *Inside Al Qaeda: Global Network of Terror*, New York: Columbia University Press, 2002, pp. 8, 10. See also "Qaeda's New Links Increase Threats from Far-Flung States," *New York Times*, June 16, 2002, and "'They're Coming After Us.' But Who Are They Now?" *New York Times*, October 20, 2002.

30. Bergen, Peter L., *Holy War, Inc.: Inside the Secret World of Osama bin Laden*, New York: The Free Press, 2001. See also Bergen, Peter L., "Al Qaeda's New Tactics," *New York Times*, November 15, 2002.

31. Gunaratna estimates that Al Qaeda's "networks are intertwined in the socio-economic, political and religious fabric of . . . at least eighty countries" (p. 10) out of the 191 (or 2, if you count Taiwan) in the world.

32. See Doran, Michael Scott, "Somebody Else's Civil War: Ideology, Rage, and the Assault on America," and Armstrong, Karen, "Was It Inevitable? Islam Through History" in Hoge, James F., Jr. and Rose, Gideon, eds., *How Did This Happen? Terrorism and the New War*, New York: Public Affairs, 2001.

33. Writing in *The National Interest*, anthropologist Robin Fox claimed that "The terrorists may well be, as [President Bush] insists, a small minority of Muslims, but they enjoy widespread sympathy and support." ("Human Rights and Foreign Policy," Number 68, Summer 2002, p. 120). But a February 2002 Gallup poll of Islamic countries revealed that the vast majority of Muslims labeled the 9/11 attacks "morally unjustifiable." Sixty-seven percent of Iranians took that position, for example, as opposed to 19 percent who found the terror justified. See Newport, Frank, "Gallup Poll of the Islamic World," Gallup Tuesday Briefing, February 26, 2002.

34. United Nations Development Programme and the Arab Fund for Economic and Social Development, *Arab Human Development Report 2002: Creating Opportunities for Future Generations.*

35. Hersh, Seymour M., "King's Ransom," *New Yorker*, October 22, 2001.

36. Transparency International 2002 Corruption Perceptions Index rates Jordan the least corrupt Arab country at a score of 4.5 (where 10 means highly clean and 0 highly corrupt) and Egypt at 3.4. Pakistan receives a 2.6 rating and Indonesia 1.9, among the lowest scorers in the world.

37. One of the great ironies of the war on terror is that many aspects of American culture that Islamic fundamentalists abhor, such as the lascivious nature of Hollywood movies and the ready availability of drugs, alcohol, and sexual stimulation, are condemned with equal vigor by Christian fundamentalists and their political allies.

38. *Op. Cit.*, Newport.

39. "Indonesians Say They suspect C.I.A. in Bali Blast," *New York Times*, November 7, 2002.

40. Kristoff, Nicholas D., "Saddam, the U.S. Agent," *New York Times*, October 15, 2002.

41. "World's View of U.S. Sours After Iraq War, Poll Finds," *New York Times,* June 4, 2003.

42. *Op. Cit.*, Gunaratna, pp. 232–233.

43. Winthrop, John, "A Model of Christian Charity," in Perry Miller, ed., *The American Puritans: Their Prose and Poetry*, Garden City, N.Y.: Doubleday & Co., 1956, p. 83.

44. Miller, Perry, *Errand into the Wilderness*, New York: Harper & Row, 1956, p. 143.

45. Quoted in Marty, Martin E., *The One and the Many*, Cambridge: Harvard University Press, 1997, p. 37.

46. Rossiter, Clinton, *The Political Thought of the American Revolution*, New York: Harcourt, Brace & World, 1963, p. 227.

47. Quoted in Becker, Carl L., *The Declaration of Independence: A Study in the History of Political Ideals*, New York: Random House, 1942, pp. 244 and 252.

48. Church, Forrest, *The American Creed: A Spiritual and Patriotic Primer*, New York: St. Martin's Press, 2002, pp. 51–52, to which I am indebted for much of this analysis.

49. Smith, Page, *John Adams, Volume II, 1784–1826*, Garden City, N.Y.: Doubleday & Co., 1962, p. 976.

50. Linfield, Michael, *Freedom Under Fire: U.S. Civil Liberties in Times of War*, Boston: South End Press, 1990, p. 27. See also Neely, Mark E., Jr., *The Fate of Liberty: Abraham Lincoln and Civil Liberties*, New York: Oxford University Press, 1991.

51. *Ibid.*, p. 44.

52. *Op. Cit.*, Church, pp. 73–74.

53. Chace, James, "Tomorrow the World," *New York Review of Books*, November 21, 2002.

54. *Op. Cit.*, Church, pp. 91–92.

55. Slavery is, of course, still practiced today in far too many corners of the globe—see Bales, Kevin, *Disposable People: New Slavery in the Global Economy*, Berkeley: University of California Press, 1999—but it is officially condemned by virtually every government (to say nothing of intergovernmental body), even those that tolerate it.

56. Lauren, Paul Gordon, *The Evolution of International Human Rights*, Philadelphia: University of Pennsylvania Press, 1998, p. 246.

57. Amnesty International, *USA: Rights for All*, 1998, p. 126.

58. Rice, Condoleeza, "Promoting the National Interest," *Foreign Affairs*, January/February 2000, p. 62.

59. Program on International Policy Attitudes, "Americans on Globalization: A Study of U.S. Public Attitudes," University of Maryland, 1999, p. 8.

60. Buchanan, Patrick J., *The Death of the West: How Dying Populations and Immigrant Invasions Imperil Our Country and Civilization*, New York: St. Martin's Press, 2002, p. 242, and Eland, Ivan, "Protecting the Homeland: The Best Defense Is to Give No Offense," Cato Policy Analysis No. 306, May 5, 1998.

61. "2000 Presidential Election—George W. Bush's Views on Defense," *National Defense*, October 1, 2000 and *Op. Cit*, Rice.

62. Armstrong, David, "Dick Cheney's Song of America," *Harper's Magazine*, October, 2002, p. 78.

63. "Statement of Principles," Project for the New American Century, June 3, 1997.

64. "Rebuilding America's Defenses: Strategy, Forces, and Resources for a New Century," Project for a New American Century, September 2000.

65. U.S. Government, *The National Security Strategy of the United States of America*, September 2002.

66. Kristol, William, and Robert Kagan, "Toward a Neo-Reaganite Foreign Policy," July/August 1996 *Foreign Affairs*, p. 20.

67. See, for example, Rumsfeld, Donald, "Transforming the Military, *Foreign Affairs*, May/June 2002, p. 31.

68. Ullman, Richard, "The US and the World: An Interview with George Kennan," *New York Review of Books*, August 12, 1999.

69. Power, Jonathan, "Henry Kissinger Should be Tried for War Crimes," http//www.taipeitimes.com/News/archives/2001/03/04/0000076137.

70. "Foreign Policy and the Republican Future," *Weekly Standard*, September 7, 1998.

71. "American Power—For What? A Symposium," *Commentary*, January 1, 2000.

72. The first statement is from a conversation with the author, December 18, 2002; the second from "The Busy Life of Being a Lightning Rod for Bush," *New York Times*, April 22, 2002.

73. "Meet the Press," September 16, 2001.

74. Quoted in Chace, James, "Imperial America and the Common Interest," *World Policy Journal*, Volume XIX, No. 1, Spring 2002, p. 5.

75. Mead, Walter Russell, "The Jacksonian Tradition and American Foreign Policy," *National Interest*, Winter 1999/2000, vol. 58, pp. 17–18.

76. Huntington, Samuel, *The Clash of Civilizations and the Remaking of the World Order*, New York: Simon & Schuster, 1996. For background, see Barry, Tom and Jim Lobe, "The Men Who Stole the Show," *Foreign Policy in Focus*, Special report No. 18, October 2002.

77. See, for example, Bolton, John, "America's Skepticism about the United Nations," *US Foreign Policy Agenda*, USIA Electronic Journal, Vol. 2, No. 2, May, 1997, and "Kofi Annan's U.N. Power Grab," *On the Issues*, American Enterprise Institute, November, 1999. The second quote is from Schulz, William F. and John Bolton, "What Price Human Rights? An Exchange," *The National Interest*, No. 56, Summer 1999, p. 113.

78. The first quote is from Worth, Robert F., "Truth, Right, and the American Way: A Nation Defines Itself by Its Evil Enemies," *New York Times*, February 24, 2002; the second from Ashcroft, John, "We Have No King But Jesus," a speech delivered May 8, 1999 at Bob Jones University, Greenville, S.C.

79. *Op. Cit.*, Winthrop, pp. 83–84.

80. Quoted in *Op. Cit.*, Rossiter, p. 200.

81. "This is not aimed at our policies," Said Henry Kissinger shortly after 9/11. "This is aimed at our existence." (Danner, Mark, "The Battlefield in the American Mind," *New York Times*, October 16, 2001.) "Arab and Muslim hatred of the United States is not just, or even mainly, a response to U.S. policies . . . ," wrote Barry Rubin of the Global Research in International Affairs Center. "Rather, such animus is largely the product of self-interested manipulation by various groups within Arab society, groups that use anti-Americanism as a foil to distract public attention from far more serious problems within those societies." ("The Real Roots of Arab Anti-Americanism," *Foreign Affairs*, November/December 2002, p. 73) While there is truth in this latter point, it does not obviate the fact that U.S. policies have provided the grist for that propaganda mill.

82. "In Search for Democracy, U.S. Is Rejected as a Guide," *New York Times*, September 28, 2002.

83. Phillips, Margaret Mann, *The "Adages" of Erasmus: A Study with Translations*, Cambridge: At the University Press, 1964, No. 317.

84. "Courage of the Morning," *Amnesty Now*, Winter 2001–2002.

85. Interview with Brzezinski, *Nouvel Observateur*, January 15–21, 1998.

86. For a critique of this perspective, see Alterman, Eric, "'Blowback,' the Prequel," *The Nation*, November 12, 2001.

87. Amnesty International, "Afghanistan: The Legacy of Human Suffering in a Forgotten War," November 1999.

88. Mishra, Pankaj, "The Making of Afghanistan," *New York Review of Books*, November 15, 2001.

89. "Bin Laden is Reported Spotted in a Fortified Camp in Eastern Afghanistan," *New York Times*, November 25, 2001.

90. "Pakistanis Fume as Clothing Sales to U.S. Tumble," *New York Times*, June 23, 2001.

91. "How Saddam Happened," *Newsweek*, September 23, 2002.

92. Amnesty International, "Torture in Iraq: 1982–84," April 1985.

93. Department of State, "Country Reports on Human Rights Practices for 1984," February 1985.

94. See Power, Samantha, *"A Problem from Hell:" America and the Age of Genocide*, New York: Basic Books, 2002, pp. 226-31.

95. "U.S. Had Key Role in Iraq Buildup," *Washington Post*, December 30, 2002; "Iraq Links Germs for Weapons to U.S. and France," *New York Times*, March 16, 2003.

96. Zumach, Andreas, "U.S.A. Censors Iraq Report," *Die Tageszeitung*, December 18, 2002.

97. *Op. Cit.*, "How Saddam Happened."

98. Human Rights Watch, "Egypt: Human Rights Background," October 2001. Alleged homosexuals are at particular risk of arrest in Egypt, as the cases of fifty-two men taken into custody for that "crime" in May 2001 attest.

99. Amnesty International, "Saudi Arabia: A Secret State of Suffering," January 2000, p. 1. See also Amnesty International, "Saudi Arabia Remains a Fertile Ground for Torture with Impunity," May 2002.

100. Amnesty International, "Gross Human Rights Abuses Against Women," September 2000.

101. A Movement in Saudi Arabia Pushes Toward an Islamic Ideal, and Frowns on the U.S.," *New York Times*, December 9, 2002.

102 Among the examples of speculation regarding instability, see Seymour Hersh, "King's Ransom," *New Yorker*, October 22, 2001, and "U.S. Pondering Saudi's Vulnerability," *New York Times*, November 4, 2001. Prince Walid ibn Talal called for elections in November, 2001 ("Saudi Prince Proposes Speedy Elections," *International Herald Tribune*, November 29, 2001, and Mohsen al-Aswaji, a dissident imprisoned for five years in the 1990s, has been allowed to travel to Qatar to appear on the Al-Jazeera television network, where he blasted the Saudi regime ("Free Radicals: In a Switch, Saudis Let Some Dissidents Speak their Minds," *Wall Street Journal*, May 9, 2002.

103. "Anger at U.S. Said to Be at New High," *New York Times*, September 11, 2002.

104. Lewis, Bernard, "The Revolt of Islam," *New Yorker*, November 19, 2001, p. 56.

105. Amnesty has forcefully and repeatedly condemned attacks on Israeli civilians. See Amnesty International, "Israel, the Occupied Territories and the Palestinian Authority: Without Distinction—Attacks on Civilians by Palestinian Armed Groups," July 2002.

106. "Confessions of a Bulldozer Driver," *Yediot Ahronot*, June 4, 2002.

107. See, for example, Amnesty International, "Israel and the Occupied Territories: The Heavy Price of Israeli Incursions," April 2002 Amnesty International, "Israel and the Occupied Territories and the Palestinian Authority: Killing the Future—Children in the Line of Fire," November 2002, Amnesty International, "Israel and the Occupied Territories: Shielded from Scrutiny: IDF violations in Jenin and Nablus," November 2002 and *B'Tselem*, "Operation Defensive Shield," 2002.

108. "New Suicide Attackers Are Rising Untrained from Anger of the Street," *New York Times*, June 21, 2002. See also Hassan, Nasra, "An Arsenal of Believers," *New Yorker*, November 19, 2001.

109. "Prisoners' Dilemmas," *Harper's Magazine*, September 2002.

110. "U.S. to Sell Military Gear to Algeria to Help It Fight Militants," *New York Times*, December 10, 2002.

111. Amnesty International, "Rights at Risk: Amnesty International's Concerns Regarding Security Legislation and Law Enforcement Measures," January 2002, p. 18.

112. President Bush subsequently designated the Uighurs' East Turkestan Islamic Movement a terrorist organization, thus sacrificing the Uighurs' traditionally benevolent view of the United States. '"U.S. Silent about China's War Against Uighurs," *Orlando Sentinel*, January 6, 2003.' China has used the U.S.-led war against terrorism as an excuse for cracking down on dissidents of all stripes, including U.S. citizen Wang Bingzhang, a prominent critic of the regime, arrested in December 2002 for "violent terrorist activity." ("China Says It Holds American-Based Dissident on Terror Charges, *New York Times*, December 22, 2002.)

113. Human Rights Watch, "Opportunism in the Face of Tragedy," September 25, 2001.

114. "U.S. Backs Oil Giant on Lawsuit in Indonesia," *New York Times*, August 8, 2002.

115. "Bribery Inquiry Involves Kazakh Chief, and He's Unhappy," *New York Times*, December 11, 2002.

116. Joint Statement by President George W. Bush and President Nursultan Nazarbayev on the new Kazakhstan-American relationship, December 21, 2001.

117. "Bush Wary of Confronting Putin," *Washington Post*, May 26, 2002.

118. Amnesty International, "Uzbekistan: The Rhetoric of Human Rights Protection: Briefing for the United Nations Human Rights Committee," June 2001.

119. Caryl, Christian, "Tyrants on the Take," *New York Review of Books*, April 11, 2002, p. 30.

120. Goldfarb, Jeffrey C., "Losing Our Best Allies in the War on Terror," *New York Times*, August 20, 2002.

121. Kristoff, Nicholas, "Why Do They Hate Us?" *New York Times*, January 15, 2002.

122. "Once a Stalwart Ally, Seoul Is Challenging U.S. Policy," *New York Times*, January 2, 2003.

123. "Humanitarian Organizations: Administration Earns 'F' on Conflict Diamond Valentine's Day," PR Newswire, February 13, 2002.

124. "Musharraf Sees Blair and Plans to Announce Steps Against Extremists," *New York Times*, January 8, 2002.

125. Cassidy, John, *New Yorker*, March 18, 2002, p. 64.

126. "U.S.: Death Penalty, Military Trials Complicating Al Qaeda Suspects' Extradition from Europe," Radio Free Europe, August 15, 2002 and "Germany Reluctant to Aid Prosecution of Moussaoui," *Washington Post* Foreign Service, June 11, 2002.

127. 8 CFR 287.3

128. Amnesty International, "USA: Amnesty International's Concerns Regarding Post September 11 Detentions in the USA," March, 2002, p. 10.

129. *Body of Principles for the Protection of All Persons Under Any Form of Detention or Imprisonment* (G. A. res. 43/173, December 9, 1988).

130. "Civil-liberties Claims Challenge Anti-terror Policy," *International Herald Tribune*, August 5, 2002.

131. Dworkin, Ronald, "The Threat to Patriotism," *New York Review of Books*, February 28, 2002.

132. Tohid, Oswald, "Pakistanis Tell of U.S. Prison Horror," http://news.bbc.co.uk/hi/english/world/americas/newsid_2074000/2074857.stm.

133. "Dozens of Israeli Jews Are Being Kept in Federal Detention," *New York Times*, November 21, 2001.

134. Gorenberg, Gershom, "A Foreigner in Solitary in America," *Washington Post*, December 8, 2001.

135. Even in times of "public emergency," the International Covenant on Civil and Political Rights, which the United States has ratified, precludes "discrimination solely on the ground of race, colour, sex, language, religion, or social origin."

136. "US Plan to Monitor Muslims Meets with Widespread Protest," *New York Times*, January 18, 2003.

an Rights in China," in Steiner, Henry J. and Philip Alston,
al Human Rights in Context: Law, Politics, Morals, Oxford:
Press, 1996, p. 233.

eservations of the United States to the ICCPR include provision
ited States is bound to observe Article 7's prohibition on "cruel,
r degrading treatment or punishment" only to the extent that it
d unusual treatment or punishment behavior prohibited by the
th or Fourteenth Amendment to the Constitution of the United
e United States has also asserted a reservation regarding the
rohibition on execution of juvenile offenders.

human rights defenders may well favor military intervention is
by Jose Ramos-Horta, the Nobel Peace Prize-winning Minister
Affairs and Cooperation from East Timor and a staunch human
cate, who editorialized strongly in favor of a United States inva-
q in order not to "keep a ruthless dictator in power." "War for
Vorked in My Country," *New York Times,* February 25, 2003.

Cit., Power, pp. 329–389. No more telling example of U.S.
nce could there be than the exchange between State
nt spokesperson Christine Shelly and Reuters correspondent
r on June 10, 1994, two months after the genocide had begun
64). Shelly is trying to distinguish between "genocide" and "acts
e," having acknowledged that the latter had occurred. "What's
nce . . . ?" Elsner asked.

ly: Well, I think the—as you know, there's a legal definition
is. . . . Clearly not all the killings . . . are killings to which
might apply that label. . . . But as to the distinction
veen the words, we're trying to call what we have seen so
s best we can, and based, again, on the evidence, we have
y reason to believe that acts of genocide have occurred.

er: How many acts of genocide does it take to make
cide?

ly: Alan, that's just not a question I'm in a position to
er.

n Rights Watch reported early and often on the crisis but had no
constituency to mobilize.

137. "U.S. Report Faults the Roundup of Illegal Aliens After 9/11," *New York Times,* June 3, 2003.

138. "A Cuban Dissident Is Defiant after Crackdown Nets Dozens," *New York Times,* March 26, 2003.

139. "Bush Administration Wins Court Victory on Guantanamo Dentions," *New York Times,* March 12, 2003.

140. "An Uneasy Routine at Cuba Prison Camp," *New York Times,* March 16, 2002.

141. "Rumsfeld Backs Plan to Hold Captives Even if Acquitted," *New York Times,* March 29, 2002.

142. "Afghans Freed from Guantanamo Speak of Heat and Isolation," *New York Times,* October 29, 2002.

143. While the United States has not ratified this protocol, the rights cited qualify as customary international law which the Supreme Court in *The Paquette Habana,* 175 US 677 (1900) obliged the United States to respect. See Neier, Aryeh, "The Military Tribunals on Trial," *New York Review of Books,* February 14, 2002.

144. Despite the fact that more than twenty alleged terrorists have been successfully prosecuted in civilian courts without compromising intelligence or putting judges or juries in danger.

145. See Dworkin, Ronald, "The Trouble with the Tribunals," *New York Review of Books,* April 25, 2002.

146. A policy the American Bar Association has decried, saying, "It is . . . paradoxical . . . that uncharged U.S. citizens [Padilla and Hamdi] have fewer rights and protections than those who have been charged with serious criminal offenses [e. g., Moussaoui]." ("ABA Opposes Bush Enemy Combatants' policy," *Los Angeles Times,* February 11, 2003.)

147. "Pentagon Says Acquittals May Not Free Detainees," *New York Times,* March 22, 2002.

148. "U.S. Decries Abuse but Defends Interrogations," *Washington Post,* December 26, 2002.

149. The Lawyers Committee for Human Rights, "A Year of Loss: Reexamining Civil Liberties Since September 11," September 5, 2002, p. 19.

150. "Bush Administration to Propose System for Wide Monitoring of Internet," *New York Times*, December 20, 2002.

151. "Muslims Protest Monthlong Detention Without a Charge," *New York Times*, April 20, 2003.

152. "U.S. Defends Secret Evidence in Charity Case," *New York Times*, October 30, 2002.

153. American Civil Liberties Union, "Insatiable Appetite: The Government's Demand for New and Unnecessary Powers After September 11," no date, p. 7.

154. "No-Fly Blacklist Snares Political Activists," *San Francisco Chronicle*, September 27, 2002.

155. "For 9/11 Hero, Humiliation; Muslim Men Report to INS," *Newsday*, November 17, 2002.

156. "Facing Registration Deadline, Men from Muslim Nations Swamp Immigration Office," *New York Times*, December 17, 2002.

157. Quoted in Als, Hilton, "Borrowed Culture," *New Yorker*, March 3, 2003, p. 88.

158. Watson, Lyall, *The Dreams of Dragons: Riddles of Natural History*, New York: William Morrow & Co., 1987.

159. See, for example, Fox, Robin, "Human Nature and Human Rights," *National Interest*, Number 62, Winter 2000–2001.

160. Fukuyama, Francis, "Natural Rights and Human History," *National Interest*, No. 64, Summer 2001.

161. Fukuyama, Francis, *Our Posthuman Future: Consequences of the Biotechnology Revolution*, New York: Farrar, Straus & Giroux, 2002, p. 173.

162. Rieff, David, *A Bed for the Night: Humanitarianism in Crisis*, New York: Simon & Schuster, 2002, pp. 8–9.

163. American Anthropological Association, "Statement on Human Rights," *American Anthropologist*, No. 4, 539, 1947.

164. For a detailed account of the process by which the UDHR was created and adopted, see Morsink, Johannes, *The Universal Declaration of Human Rights: Origins, Drafting & Intent*, Philadelphia: The University of Pennsylvania Press, 1999.

165. One hundred forty-four countries have Covenant on Civil and Political Rights, 142 the Social, Cultural and Economic Rights, 156 the I the Elimination of Racial Discrimination, 191 th of the Child.

166. An-na'im, Abdullah Ahmed, "Human Right Steiner, Henry J. and Alston, Philip, *Intern Context: Law, Politics, Morals*, Oxford: Clarend

167. Sen, Amartya, "Human Rights and Asian Va Council on Ethics and International Affairs, 199

168. "In a Contest of Cultures, East Embrace March 12, 2003.

169. They are also offering insight into discipli rationalism of the West whereby human rights second nature, states of being related to equanim sion in response to the suffering of others. Ann how this comes to be in a Buddhist context (se *Queen*, Boston: Beacon Press, 1995, pp. 89–93.) Sharon Welch for this insight.

170. Dworkin, Ronald, "Taking Rights Serious *Review of Books*, September 26, 2002, p. 65.

171. Wills, Garry, *Confessions of a Conserv* Doubleday & Co., 1979, pp. 155–56.

172. For a comprehensive discussion of all aspect see Shell-Duncan, Bettina and Ylva Hernlund, *Africa: Culture, Controversy, and Change*, Publishers, 2000. Educational campaigns are chan FGC among a younger generation. See "Af Denounce Genital Cutting," *New York Times*, Fe

173. *Op. Cit.*, Fukuyama, "Human Rights and Hu

174. *The Weekly Standard*, June 2001.

175. Palmer, R. R. and Joel Colton, *A History of* York: Alfred A., Knopf, 1965, p. 123.

176. "Hu *Internati* Clarendo

177. The that the inhuman is "cruel Fifth, Ei States." ICCPR's

178. Tha illustrate of Foreig rights ad sion of I Peace? I

179. *Op* intransi Departn Alan Els (pp. 363 of geno the diffe

S o y b fa e

E g *S* a

180. H grassro

181. Oppenheim, Lassa, *International Law*, vol. 1, New York: Longmans, Green & Co., 1948 (first published 1905), p. 279.

182. "We Were Calling to Death," *Harper's Magazine*, February 2003, pp. 14–15.

183. Annan, Kofi, "Two Concepts of Sovereignty," *Economist*, September 18, 1999.

184. Report of the International Commission on Intervention and State Sovereignty, The Responsibility to Protect, Ottawa: International Development Research Center, 2001, p. 13.

185. See Schulz, William F., *In Our Own Best Interests: How Defending Human Rights Benefits Us All,* Boston: Beacon Press, 2001.

186. General Dallaire has suffered deep personal distress about his inability to stop the killing in Rwanda, a poignant story that is told in Allen, Terry J., "The General and the Genocide," *Amnesty NOW*, Winter 2002.

187. "Humanitarian Intervention: Crafting a Workable Doctrine," New York: Council on Foreign Relations, 2000, pp. 49–50. "We forget . . . ," Zakheim goes on, "that for the better part of a century after our independence we tolerated slavery in our midst, that the precious right to vote was granted to all citizens only in the previous century . . ." and that is true. But it is also true that history provides lessons in progress and that today's would-be democracies need not emulate our mistakes but learn from them. That the U.S.'s history is flawed is no excuse for others' current choices to be also. Following that logic, contemporary nations ought to have no truck with airplanes simply because the United States had no such contraptions 150 years ago.

188. *Op. Cit.*, "The Responsibility to Protect," p. 32.

189. Kagan, Robert, *Of Paradise and Power: America Versus Europe in the New World Order,* New York: Knopf, 2003

190. "U.S. Role in the World Dominates Economic Talks as Brazilian Clamors to Be Heard," *New York Times*, January 24, 2003.

191. Ball, Howard, *Prosecuting War Crimes and Genocide: The Twentieth Century Experience*, Lawrence, Kans.: University of Kansas Press, 1999, pp. 23–24.

192. Willis, James F., *Prologue to Nuremberg: The Politics and Diplomacy of Punishing War Criminals in the First World War*, Westport, Conn.: Greenwood Press, 1982, p. 68.

193. Singer, Peter, *One World: The Ethics of Globalization*, New Haven: Yale University Press, 2002, p. 7.

194. Moynihan, Daniel Patrick, *Pandaemonium: Ethnicity in International Politics*, Oxford: Oxford University Press, 1993, p. 72.

195. Lemann, Nicholas, "After Iraq," *New Yorker*, February 17 and 24, 2003, p. 72.

196. *Op. Cit.*, Phillips, No. 343.

197. Convention against Torture and Other Cruel, Inhuman, and Degrading Treatment or Punishment, Articles 1 and 3.

198. Alter, Jonathan, "Time to Think About Torture," *Newsweek*, November 5, 2001.

199. Hoffman, Bruce, "A Nasty Business," *Atlantic Monthly*, January 2002.

200. See Dershowitz, Alan, *Shouting Fire: Civil Liberties in a Turbulent Age*, Boston: Little, Brown, 2002, and *Why Terrorism Works: Understanding the Threat, Responding to the Challenge*, New Haven: Yale University Press, 2002.

201. "Silence of 4 Terror Probe Suspects Poses Dilemma," *Washington Post*, October 21, 2001.

202. "Quiet Shipping of Terror Suspects to Mideast Raises Query on Torture," *Christian Science Monitor*, July 26, 2002.

203. "U.S. Decries Abuse but Defends Interrogations," *Washington Post*, December 26, 2003. Many of these charges were confirmed in an interview with a prisoner released from U.S. custody at Bagram. ("Interrogation Criticized; U.S. Detainee Says He Was Forced to Strip," *Seattle Times*, March 16, 2003.)

204. "Questioning Terror Suspects in a Dark and Surreal World," *New York Times*, March 9, 2003.

205. "Army Probing Deaths of 2 Afghan Prisoners," *Washington Post*, March 5, 2003.

206. "Bush Assures U.N. Rights Boss U.S. Not Using Torture," Reuters, March 7, 2003. Finally on June 26, 2003, after prodding from human rights executives, the administration declared that the U.S. would neither torture prisoners, nor subject them to "cruel and unusual punishment." (Statement by the President, U.N. International Day in Support of Victims of Torture.)

207. The U.S. State Department Country Report on Human Rights Practices for 2002, for example, had denounced hooding, holding prisoners in prolonged painful positions, and the denial of food and sleep in such countries as Iran, Saudi Arabia, Turkey, China, and Haiti.

208. Gallup/CNN/USA Today poll, October 5–6, 2001.

209. Snepp, Frank, *Decent Interval: An Insider's Account of Saigon's Indecent End Told by the C.I.A.'s Chief Strategy Analyst in Vietnam*, New York: Random House, 1977, p. 14.

210. "Ends, Means and Barbarity," *Economist*, January 11, 2003.

211. Article 3 of the Convention against Torture states that "No State Party shall expel, return, or extradite a person to another state where there are substantial grounds for believing that he would be in danger of being subjected to torture. . . . "

212. Chace, James, "Tomorrow the World," *New York Review of Books*, November 21, 2002.

213. "Unease Grows in Philippines on U.S. Forces," *New York Times*, January 19, 2002.

214. "Plan for U.S. Troops in Philippines Hits Snag," *New York Times*, March 1, 2003. "The wounds over the massacre of our forefathers by the American colonialists have never healed," said one Filipino ("Filipinos Awaiting Us Troops with Skepticism," *New York Times*, February 28, 2003.)

215. See, for example, Aussaresses, Paul, *Special Services Algeria: 1955–57*, Perrin, 2001.

216. *Op. Cit.*, Hoffman.

217. "The Case Against Torture," *Village Voice*, November 28–December 4, 2001.

218. "Time to Torture?" Salon.com, November 16, 2001.

219. Winik, Jay, "Security Comes Before Liberty," *Wall Street Journal*, October 23, 2001.

220. A point made by William J. Aceves in "Is Torture Worth the Price of Cost-Benefit Analysis?" *San Diego Union Tribune*, November 21, 2001.

221. *Op. Cit.*, "The Case Against Torture."

222. *Op. Cit.*, Hoffman.

223. "60 Minutes," January 20, 2002.

224. "U.S. Walks a Fine Line to Make Prisoners Talk," *Toronto Globe and Mail*, September 17, 2002.

225. "U.S. Ships Al Qaeda Suspects to Arab States," *Christian Science Monitor*, July 26, 2002.

226. *Ibid*.

227. "Borderless Network of Terror; Bin Laden Followers Reach Across Globe," *Washington Post*, September 23, 2001.

228. "Captives; Rumsfeld Defends Treatment by U.S. of Cuban Detainees," *New York Times*, January 22, 2002.

229. "Lawyers Renew Plea to Meet Terror Suspect in Navy Brig," *New York Times*, January 16, 2003.

230. Whitcomb, Christopher, "The Shadow War," *Gentlemen's Quarterly*, January, 2002.

231. "Interrogations Mix Science and Art," *San Francisco Chronicle*, September 22, 2002.

232. Dershowitz, Alan, "Want to Torture? Get a Warrant," *The San Francisco Chronicle*, January 22, 2002.

233. *Op. Cit.*, Dershowitz, *Shouting Fire*, p. 477.

234. Report to the United Nations Committee Against Torture, 1999.

235. "Manila Road to Salvation Brings Huge Traffic Jams," *Boston Globe*, December 29, 1994.

236. 22 U. S. C. 2656f (d). The United Nations General Assembly has defined terrorism as "criminal acts intended or calculated to provoke a state of terror in the general public, a group of persons or particular persons for political purposes . . . whatever the considerations. . . that may be invoked to justify them." (See Talbott, Strobe, and Nayan Chanda, eds., *The Age of Terror: America and the World After September 11*, New York: Basic Books, 2001, p. 148.)

237. Takeyh, Ray, "Two Cheers from the Islamic World" *Foreign Policy*, January/February, 2002, p. 70.

238. Not all human rights groups, however, have had such compunctions. The International Commission of Jurists, for example, issued an immediate condemnation of the 9/11 attacks, saying, "These acts of terrorism constitute a vicious and malicious violation of a world order based on peace, justice, fundamental human rights, and the rule of law." (September 14, 2001) And the UN Security Council had no reservations using the term "terrorism" to condemn what happened on September 11 in its unanimously adopted resolutions 1368 (September 12, 2001) and 1373 (September 28, 2001).

239. "Argentine Junta Felt Safe from the US," *New York Times*, August 22, 2002.

240. "Will the Real Terrorist Please Stand?" *Washington Times*, July 7, 2002.

241. "South Carolina High Court Derails Video Poker Game," *New York Times*, October 15, 1999.

242. And in some legal instruments, it is not even all that vague. The International Convention for Suppressing of the Financing of Terrorism" defines terrorism in Article 2(b) as "Any . . . act intended to cause death or serious bodily injury to a civilian, or to any other person not taking an active part in hostilities in a situation of armed conflict, when the purpose of such act, by its nature and context, is to intimidate a population, or to compel a government or an international organization to do or to abstain from doing any act."

243. For a discussion of this issue, see Ignatieff, Michael, "Human Rights, the Laws of War, and Terror," *Social Research*, vol. 69, No. 4 (Winter 2002).

244. Other human rights treaties have similar provisions. The American Convention on Human Rights declares that "In time of war, public danger

or other emergency that threatens the independence or security of a State Party, it may take measures derogating from its obligations under the . . . Convention" but then excepts eleven articles of the Convention that can never be modified or suspended. The European Convention on Human Rights regards four of its articles as non-derogable. For purposes of our discussion, we will track the provisions of the ICCPR, however, because, of the three treaties, it has been ratified by the largest number of nations.

245. See Zakaria, Fareed, *The Future of Freedom: Illiberal Democracy at Home and Abroad*, New York: W. W. Norton & Co., 2003.

246. Fitzpatrick, Joan, *Human Rights in Crisis: The International System for Protecting Rights during States of Emergency*, Philadelphia: University of Pennsylvania Press, 1994, pp. 56–57.

247. "U.S. to Appeal Order Giving Lawyers Access to Detainee," *New York Times*, March 26, 2003.

248. Ironically enough, it was the United States (and France) that proposed during the preparation of the ICCPR that the prohibition on arbitrary arrest, the right to prompt notice of charges and the right to fair and prompt trial be nonderogable. The UK objected and its view prevailed. See *Op. Cit.*, Fitzpatrick, p. 39, footnote 45.

249. "Police Stop Collecting Data on Protesters' Politics," *New York Times*, April 10, 2003.

250. "Interviews of Visa Holders Yield Little So Far," *The Washington Post*, December 8, 2001.

251. The American Convention says rights may be derogated "for the period of time strictly required by the exigencies of the situation" (Article 27).

252. "F.B.I. Tells Offices to Count Local Muslims and Mosques," *New York Times*, January 29, 2003.

253. Quoted in Mailer, Norman, "Only in America," *New York Review of Books*, March 27, 2003.

254. Robertson, Frank, "Letters," *Dharma World*, November/December 2002.

255. Pew Research Center, "What the World Thinks in 2002: How Global Publics View: Their Lives, Their Countries, the World, America," December 4, 2002.

256. Quoted in Friedman, Thomas L., "Under the Arab Street," *New York Times*, October 23, 2002.

257. "Talk of Arab 'Democracy' Is a Doubled-Edged Scimitar," *New York Times*, February 28, 2003.

258. "Ranking the Rich," *Foreign Policy*, May/June 2003.

259. Dershowitz, Alan, *Why Terrorism Works*, New Haven: Yale University Press, pp. 24–25

260. Friedman, Thomas L., "The New Math," *The New York Times*, January 15, 2003.

261. "A Diplomatic Star With a Singular Style," *New York Times*, January 20, 2002.

262. April 25, 2003.

263. Dominus, Susan, "Their Day in Court," *New York Times Magazine*, March 30, 2003, p. 33.

264. Kaplan, Robert D., *Warrior Politics: Why Leadership Demands a Pagan Ethos*, New York: Random House, 2002, pp. 21, 146-47, and 109.

265. From Fenyvesi, Charles, *When the World Was Whole*, New York: Viking.

INDEX

Index

Index